D1555494

ALIEN PHENOMENOLOGY,
OR WHAT IT'S LIKE
TO BE A THING

Cary Wolfe, Series Editor

Alien Phenomenology,
or What It's Like
to Be a Thing

IAN BOGOST

posthumanities **20**

UNIVERSITY OF MINNESOTA PRESS

MINNEAPOLIS • LONDON

Portions of the book were previously published as "The Phenomenology of Videogames," in *Proceedings of the Philosophy of Computer Games Conference*, ed. Stephan Günzel, Michael Leibe, and Dieter Mersch (Potsdam: Universitätsverlag Potsdam, 2008), 22–43.

"Particle Man," words and music by John Linnell and John Flansburgh. Copyright 1991 TMBG Music. All rights on behalf of TMBG Music administered by Warner-Tamerlane Publishing Corporation. All rights reserved. Used by permission of Alfred Music Publishing Company, Inc.

"Waters of March," original text and music by Antônio Carlos Jobim. Copyright 1972.

"16-bit Intel 8088 Chip" from *You Get So Alone at Times That It Just Makes Sense*, by Charles Bukowski. Copyright 1986 by Linda Lee Bukowski. Reprinted by permission of HarperCollins Publisher.

Copyright 2012 by Ian Bogost

All rights reserved. No part of this publication may be reproduced, stored in a retrieval system, or transmitted, in any form or by any means, electronic, mechanical, photocopying, recording, or otherwise, without the prior written permission of the publisher.

Published by the University of Minnesota Press
111 Third Avenue South, Suite 290
Minneapolis, MN 55401-2520
http://www.upress.umn.edu

Design by Yvonne Tsang at Wilsted & Taylor Publishing Services

Library of Congress Cataloging-in-Publication Data
Bogost, Ian.
Alien phenomenology, or What it's like to be a thing / Ian Bogost.
(Posthumanities ; 20)
Includes bibliographical references and index.
ISBN 978-0-8166-7897-6 (hc : alk. paper)
ISBN 978-0-8166-7898-3 (pb : alk. paper)
1. Ontology. 2. Metaphysics. 3. Phenomenology.
I. Title. II. Title: What it's like to be a thing.
BD331.B5927 2012
111—dc23   2012001202

Printed in the United States of America on acid-free paper

The University of Minnesota is an equal-opportunity educator and employer.

20   19   18   17   16   15   14   13   10   9   8   7   6   5   4   3

Particle man, particle man
Doing the things a particle can
What's he like? It's not important
Particle man

Is he a dot, or is he a speck?
When he's underwater does he get wet?
Or does the water get him instead?
Nobody knows, Particle man

—They Might Be Giants, "Particle Man"

CONTENTS

[1]

ALIEN PHENOMENOLOGY

New Mexico offered me a childhood of weird objects.

When the weather is clear, the Sandia Mountains to the east of Albuquerque drip the juices of their namesake fruit for a spell each evening, ripening quickly until the twilight devours them. At the range's southern foothill, apple trees take the place of watermelons. There, in the hollowed-out Manzano Mountain, the U.S. Armed Forces Special Weapons Command once stashed the nation's largest domestic nuclear weapons repository, some 2,450 warheads as of the turn of the millennium.[1]

One hundred miles due south from the Sandias rests Trinity Site. There, in the summer of 1944, Edward Teller, Enrico Fermi, and Robert Oppenheimer placed dollar wagers on the likelihood that testing an implosion-design plutonium device would ignite the atmosphere. Today, the site opens to the public on the first Saturdays of April and October. Families caravan in from the nearby cities of Socorro and Alamogordo to picnic on roast beef and roentgens.

At the southern edge of the Sangre de Cristos, down which blood runs at dusk instead of nectar, different munitions lay buried beneath Sharpshooter's Ridge: buckshot from Union buck-and-ball muskets of the 1862 Battle of Glorieta Pass.

It's a small sample of the world that sat unconsidered beneath, above, around, behind, and before me: mountains, fruit, atmospheric effects, nuclear warheads, sandwiches, automobiles, historical events, relics. A few entries logged in the register of one tiny corner of the universe.

Yet no catalog of New Mexico would be complete without the

aliens. Two short years after Oppenheimer incanted from the Bhaga-vad Gita at the fireball that would ignite suburbia, Roswell Army Air Field personnel allegedly recovered a crashed flying saucer, as well as the bodies of its anthropomorphic passengers. In the reports and conspiracy theories that followed, the craft, corpses, and debris were often called "nothing made on this earth," although each ele-ment remained conveniently identifiable as spacecraft, equipment, or invader.[2]

Roswell's are the aliens who looked for us. West of Socorro, we look for them. There, amid the desolate plains of the San Agustin Basin, lounge the twenty-seven antennas of the Very Large Array (VLA). They stretch twenty-five meters across and point up toward the big, blue sky like so many steel calderas. When linked like a school of tropical fish, the VLA antenna is used for various experi-ments in astrophysics, including the study of black holes, supernovas, and nearby galaxies. But many prefer to think that the occasional use of the array by organizations like the Search for Extraterrestrial Intel-ligence (SETI) constitutes the primary purpose of the instruments. Radio telescopes listen to the sky; SETI collects and analyzes the data in a hopeful search for electromagnetic transmissions suggestive of extraterrestrial life.[3] It's a field called astrobiology, one unique in the research community for possessing not a single confirmed object of study.

Meanwhile, to the northeast of the buried buckshot at Glorieta Pass, past the mountains whose crests draw the blood of Christ, be-yond the ski resorts and the hippie enclaves and the celebrity ranches lies the Raton-Clayton field, where the corpses of hundreds of vol-canic scoria cones laugh silently at the fatuous trendiness of both musket and plutonium, as they have done for the fifty thousand years since their last eruption.[4]

To the south, across the field's cousin lava flows at Carrizozo Mal-pais, beyond the Trinity Site, the gypsum dunes of White Sands shift in the wind. Like a Žižekian daydream, they form a seashore that stretches across 275 square miles without ever reaching the sea. Once an alternate landing site for another tool to study the cosmos, the space shuttle, that vessel landed here only once, on March 30, 1982.[5] The cleanup proved too onerous, as NASA was forced to extract gypsum from every last crevice of the Columbia's body, like a nurse-maid might do to a corpulent boy after a raucous day at the beach. When the spaceship shattered silently over Texas twenty-one years later, the White Sands gypsum still shifted, going nowhere.

Just to the west, in Doña Ana County, the hot, dry sun increases capsaicin levels in the green chile crops that grow around the tiny village of Hatch. Tumbling in vented steel cylinders, chiles crackle over the open flame of roasting. Eventually their skins blister and brown, then blacken. Peel separates to reveal the bright green meat beneath, as if drawn open like the wounds of the mountain-Christ. They cover plates of enchiladas as shrubs cover the hundreds of square miles of their high desert home.

THE STATE OF THINGS

Why do we give the dead Civil War soldier, the guilty Manhattan project physicist, the oval-headed alien anthropomorph, and the intelligent celestial race so much more credence than the scoria cone, the obsidian fragment, the gypsum crystal, the capsicum pepper, and the propane flame? When we welcome these things into scholarship, poetry, science, and business, it is only to ask how they relate to human productivity, culture, and politics. We've been living in a tiny prison of our own devising, one in which all that concerns us are the fleshy beings that are our kindred and the stuffs with which we stuff ourselves. Culture, cuisine, experience, expression, politics, polemic: all existence is drawn through the sieve of humanity, the rich world of things discarded like chaff so thoroughly, so immediately, so efficiently that we don't even notice. How did it come to this, an era in which "things" means ideas so often, and stuff so seldom? A brief excursion into philosophy's recent past reveals the source of our conceit.

Consider the legacy of Immanuel Kant's transcendental idealism. The views we inherit at Kant's bequest are so prevalent that they lie unseen and unquestioned—like the mountains and the gypsum and the watermelons.

Being, this position holds, exists only for subjects. In George Berkeley's subjective idealism, objects are just bundles of sense data in the minds of those who perceive them. In G. W. F. Hegel's absolute idealism, the world is best characterized by the way it appears to the self-conscious mind. For Martin Heidegger, objects *are* outside human consciousness, but their *being* exists only in human understanding. For Jacques Derrida, things are never fully present to us, but only differ and defer their access to individuals in particular contexts, interminably. This is but a small sample that dog-ears a much longer history of modern philosophy, just as the catalog above accounts for only a tiny fraction of the things that bake under the hot New Mexico sun.

All such moves consider being a problem of access, and human access at that. Quentin Meillassoux has coined the term *correlationism* to describe this view, one that holds that being exists only as a correlate between mind and world.[6] If things exist, they do so only *for us*. Meillassoux offers a characteristic example: the correlationist cannot accept a statement like "Event Y occurred x number of years before the emergence of humans."

> No—he will simply add—perhaps only to himself, but add it he will—something like a simple codicil, always the same one, which he will discreetly append to the end of the phrase: event Y occurred x number of years before the emergence of humans—for humans (or even, for the human scientist).[7]

In the correlationist's view, humans and the world are inextricably tied together, the one never existing without the other. Meillassoux offers a censure akin to Bruno Latour's critique of modernity: theory has attempted to split the world into two halves, *human* and *nature*.[8] Human culture is allowed to be multifarious and complex, but the natural or material world is only ever permitted to be singular.

Thanks to the title of a symposium at Goldsmith's College in 2007, Meillassoux has been tentatively housed with Ray Brassier, Iain Hamilton Grant, and Graham Harman under the philosophical shingle "speculative realism." But this title does little to unite the different positions of these four thinkers, which range from neomaterialism to neonihilism.[9] The speculative realists share a common position less than they do a common enemy: the tradition of human access that seeps from the rot of Kant. Even if tales of Kant's infamous introversion are overstated, they are true enough to have birthed this irony: the blinkered state of philosophy-as-access arrives on the coattails of a man who never strayed far from the Prussian town of Königsberg. For more than two centuries, philosophy has remained mousy and reticent, a recluse.

Fleeing from the dank halls of the mind's prison toward the grassy meadows of the material world, speculative realism must also make good on the first term of its epithet: metaphysics need not seek verification, whether from experience, physics, mathematics, formal logic, or even reason. The successful invasion of realist speculation ends the reigns of both transcendent insight and subjective incarceration.

This is just a starting point, an ante: to proceed as a philosopher today demands the rejection of correlationism. To be a speculative realist, one must abandon the belief that human access sits at the center of being, organizing and regulating it like an ontological watchmaker. In both a figurative and a literal sense, speculative realism is an *event* rather than a philosophical position: it names a moment when the epistemological tide ebbed, revealing the iridescent shells of realism they had so long occluded.[10] Like the Big Bang in cosmological theory, the philosophical event known as speculative realism inaugurates a condition of new opportunities that demonstrate the quaintness of philosophies of access.

Many more speculative realisms are sure to come, but of the positions first offered by the four horsemen of anticorrelationism, Harman's suits me best. Unlike the others, Harman most explicitly embraces the multifarious complexity of being among all things. Reality is reaffirmed, and humans are allowed to live within it alongside the sea urchins, kudzu, enchiladas, quasars, and Tesla coils.

With Heidegger's tool analysis as his raw material, Harman constructs what he calls an *object-oriented philosophy.*[11] Very quickly: Heidegger suggests that things are impossible to understand as such. Instead, they are related to purposes, a circumstance that makes speaking of harmonicas or tacos *as things* problematic; stuff becomes ready-to-hand (or *zuhanden*) when contextualized, and present-at-hand (or *vorhanden*) when it breaks from those contexts. Heidegger's favorite example is the hammer, which affords the activity of nail driving, something we look past in pursuit of a larger project, say building a house—unless it breaks and becomes abstracted.[12]

Harman argues that this "tool-being" is a truth of all objects, not just of *Dasein*: hammer, human, haiku, and hot dog are all ready-to-hand and present-at-hand for one another as much as they are for us. There is something that recedes—always hidden, inside, inaccessible.[13] He suggests that objects do not relate merely through human use but through any use, including all relations between one object and any other. Harman's position also offers an implicit rejoinder against scientific naturalism: things are not just their most basic components, be they quarks or neurons. Instead, stuffs enjoy equal being no matter their size, scale, or order.

If ontology is the philosophical study of existence, then from Harman we can derive an *object-oriented ontology* (or OOO for short—call it "triple O" for style's sake).[14] OOO puts *things* at the center of being. We humans are elements, but not the sole elements, of philosophical interest. OOO contends that nothing has special status, but that everything exists equally—plumbers, cotton, bonobos, DVD players, and sandstone, for example. In contemporary thought, things are usually taken either as the aggregation of ever smaller bits (scientific naturalism) or as constructions of human behavior and society (social relativism). OOO steers a path between the two, drawing attention to things at all scales (from atoms to alpacas, bits to blinis) and pondering their nature and relations with one another as much with ourselves.[15]

You might notice the similarities between OOO's objects and other philosophical concepts, such as Alfred North Whitehead's *occasions* in process philosophy or Latour's *actors* in actor-network theory. Such comparisons have merit, and indeed one simple way to summarize the position is to cite the informal addition Harman offers to Lee Braver's types of realism: "The human/world relation is just a special case of the relation between any two entities whatsoever," a test that both Whitehead and Latour would easily pass.[16]

Yet OOO is not the same as process philosophy or actor-network theory. For Whitehead, entities do not persist but continuously give way to one another—metaphysics amounts to change, dynamism, and flux, properties that are perhaps better known in Continental philosophy via Henri Bergson or Gilles Deleuze. The successive actual occasions of experience amount to an undermining of objects into more basic components that perish immediately, an approach I want to avoid.[17] Unlike Whitehead, Latour allows for the uncontroversial existence of things at all scales. But in the networks of actor-network theory, things remain in motion far more than they do at rest. As a result, entities are de-emphasized in favor of their couplings and decouplings. Alliances take center stage, and things move to the wings. As Latour says, "Actors do not stand still long enough to take a group photo."[18] But yet they *do*, even as they also assemble and disband from their networks. The scoria cone and the green chile remain, even as they partake of systems of plate tectonics, enchiladas, tourism, or digestion.

From the perspective of cultural theory instead of philosophy, the OOO strain of speculative realism might bear some resemblance to more familiar arguments against anthropocentrism (such as posthumanism). Environmental philosophy, for example, has argued that humankind is to ecology as man is to feminism or Anglo-Saxonism is to race. And such activists as Dave Forman have argued for the relevance of forest and wildlife as equal in status to humans.[19]

But posthuman approaches still preserve humanity as a primary actor. Either our future survival motivates environmental concern, or natural creatures like kudzu and grizzly bears are meant to be elevated *up* to the same status as humanity. In every conception of environmental holism from John Muir to James Lovelock, all beings are given equal absolute value and moral right to the planet—so long as they are indeed living creatures. One type of existence—life—still comprises the reference point for thought and action. In Latour's words, political ecology "claims to defend nature for nature's sake—and not as a substitute for human egotism—but in every instance, the mission it has assigned itself is carried out by humans and is justified by the well-being, the pleasure, or the good conscience of a small number of carefully selected humans."[20] Latour sees not one nature but many natures, each with its own identity in a collective whole. Yet even for Latour, analysis still serves the interests of human politics (to wit: the subtitle of the book from which the above quote is taken is "How to Bring the Sciences into Democracy").

In ecological discourse, an alternative perspective might look more like the one the journalist Alan Weisman offers in his book *The World without Us*.[21] Weisman documents the things that would take place if humans were to suddenly vanish from earth. Subways flood; pipes cool and crack; insects and weather slowly devour the wood frames of homes; the steel columns of bridges and skyscrapers corrode and buckle. The object-oriented position holds that we do not have to wait for the rapturous disappearance of humanity to attend to plastic and lumber and steel.

Like environmental philosophy, animal studies expands our domain of inquiry, but again it stops short by focusing on a single domain of "familiar" actants—dogs, pigs, birds, and so forth—entities routinized thanks to their similarity in form and behavior to human beings. As Richard Nash and Ron Broglio have put it, "Scholars in animal studies have increasingly turned to . . . describing the relationships between particular humans and particular animals while taking into account the culture in which both find themselves embedded."[22] Once more, we find a focus on creatures from the vantage point of human intersubjectivity, rather than from the weird, murky mists of the really real.

We might also question animal studies' arbitrary specificity. Why trees and sea turtles instead of minerals or stem and leaf succulents? As Steven Shaviro has said in a passing criticism of the zoocentrism animal studies exhibits, "What about plants, fungi, protists, bacteria, etc.?"[23] As an alternative, Michael Pollan has offered an attempt at a plant's-eye view of the world, one that grants the potato and the cannabis at least as much subjectivity as the dog or the raven. But he too seeks to valorize the apple or the potato only to mobilize them in critiques of the human practices of horticulture, nutrition, and industrialism.[24] Such critique serves and recommends cooperative practices of biodiversity, a value whose explicit purpose is to extend human life and well-being. Posthumanism, we might conclude, is not posthuman enough.

Let me be clear: we need not discount human beings to adopt an object-oriented position—after all, we ourselves are of the world as much as musket buckshot and gypsum and space shuttles. But we can no longer claim that our existence is special *as existence*.

This is true *even if* humans also possess a seemingly unique ability to agitate the world, or at least our corner of it (although this too is a particularly grandiose assumption, given that humans interact with only a tiny sliver of the universe). If we take seriously the idea that all objects recede interminably into themselves, then human perception becomes just one among many ways that objects might relate. To put things at the center of a new metaphysics also requires us to admit that they do not exist just for us.

THE COMPUTER AS PROMPT

I've been fortunate. I arrived at the metaphysics of things by way of inanimacy rather than life—from the vantage point of a critic and creator of computational media in general and videogames in particular. This perspective has been a productive one, since the subterranean dimensions of the objects with which I often surround myself do not blink with doe eyes or satisfy with macronutrients. They may facilitate work and play, but computers do not fill one's nostrils with the crisp scent of morning or ruffle one's feet with evening purrs. Unlike redwoods and lichen and salamanders, computers don't carry the baggage of vivacity. They are plastic and metal corpses with voodoo powers.

But anyone who has ever had to construct, repair, program, or otherwise operate on a computational apparatus knows that a strange and unique world does stir within such a device. A tiny, private universe rattles behind its glass and aluminum exoskeleton. Computers are composed of molded plastic keys and controllers, motor-driven disc drives, silicon wafers, plastic ribbons, and bits of data. They are likewise formed from subroutines and middleware libraries compiled into byte code or etched onto silicon, cathode ray tubes or LCD displays mated to insulated, conductive cabling, and microprocessors executing machine instructions that enter and exit address buses. I have wondered what goes on in that secret universe, too, just as much as I wonder at the disappearing worlds of the African elephant or the Acropora coral. What's it like to be a computer, or a microprocessor, or a ribbon cable?

To be sure, computers often *do* entail human experience and perception. The human operator views words and images rendered on a display, applies physical forces to a mouse, seats memory chips into motherboard sockets. But not always. Indeed, for the computer to operate at all *for us* first requires a wealth of interactions to take place *for itself.* As operators or engineers, we may be able to describe how such objects and assemblages *work.* But what do they *experience*? What's their proper phenomenology? In short, what is it like to be a thing? If we wish to understand a microcomputer or a mountain range or a radio astronomy observatory or a thermonuclear weapon or a capsaicinoid on its own terms, what approaches might be of service?

Science studies might be one answer, but that field retains some human agent at the center of analysis—usually a scientist or engineer. Latour is guilty of it, even if his own philosophical approach to actants in "Irreductions" happily brackets human actors when appropriate. Perhaps more importantly, actor-network theory has been primarily adopted as an inspiration for the study of science as a human conceit, one in need of policing and critique. A worthwhile pursuit though it may be, it tells us little of the inner worlds of Erlenmeyer flasks or rubber-tired Métro rolling stock.

Similar troubles plague vitalist and panpsychist approaches. The "akinness" of various material behaviors to human thought and feeling has promise, but it also draws far too much attention to the similarities between humans and objects, rather than their differences. Whitehead was careful to distinguish *prehension* from *consciousness,* while still managing to hold that entities are "throbs of experience."[25] David Ray Griffin has offered a helpful shorthand for this position, calling it *panexperientialism* instead of panpsychism, and the former name may suit my purposes better than the latter.[26]

Timothy Morton rightly calls vitalism a compromise, one that imprecisely projects a living nature onto all things.[27] With this in mind, Morton suggests *mesh* instead of *nature* to describe "the interconnectedness of all living and non-living things."[28] But to take such interconnectedness seriously, we must really mean it. The philosophical subject must cease to be limited to humans and things that influence humans. Instead it must become *everything,* full stop. Silicon microprocessors and data transmission ribbons are not like wild boars and black truffles. They are weird yet ordinary, unfamiliar yet human-crafted, animate but not living, just as much like limestone deposits as like kittens. In a world of panexperiential meshes, how do things have experiences?

Harman's answer is "vicarious causation."[29] Things never really interact with one another, but fuse or connect in a conceptual fashion unrelated to consciousness. These means of interaction remain unknown—we can conclude only that some kind of proxy breaks the chasm and fuses the objects without actually fusing them. Harman uses the analogy of a jigsaw puzzle: "Instead of mimicking the original image, [it] is riddled with fissures and strategic overlaps that place everything in a new light."[30] We understand relation by tracing the fissures.

But the fissures between what? Before putting vicarious causation to practical use, we must pause to ask what being is in the first place. What do we find in the mesh of possible experience? What is a thing, and what things exist?

FLAT ONTOLOGY

In short, *all things equally exist, yet they do not exist equally.* The funeral pyre is not the same as the aardvark; the porceletta shell is not equivalent to the rugby ball. Not only is neither pair reducible to human encounter, but also neither is reducible to the other.

This maxim may seem like a tautology—or just a gag. It's certainly not the sort of qualified, reasoned, hand-wrung ontological position that's customary in philosophy. But such an extreme take is required for the curious garden of things to flower. Consider it a thought experiment, as all speculation must be: what if we shed all criteria whatsoever and simply hold that everything exists, even the things that don't? And further, what if we held that among extants, none exist differently from one another? The unicorn and the combine harvester, the color red and methyl alcohol, quarks and corrugated iron, Amelia Earhart and dyspepsia, all are fair game, none's existence fundamentally different from another, none more primary nor more original.

There ought to be no need to say more or less than this, although some initial clarification is in order. This ontology is not a Parmenidean monism; existence is not singular and unchangeable. Yet it is not a Democritean atomism; existence is not composed of fundamental elements of equal size and nature. Yet once more, it is not an abstruse and undefined indeterminacy, like the lumpy Levinasian *il y a* or the undistinguished Anaximandrean *apeiron*. Instead, things can *be* many and various, specific and concrete, while their *being* remains identical.

Levi Bryant calls it *flat ontology*. He borrows the term from Manuel DeLanda, who uses it to claim that existence is composed entirely of individuals (rather than species and genera, for example).[31] Bryant uses the phrase somewhat differently: his flat ontology grants all objects the same ontological status. For Bryant (as for Latour), the term *object* enjoys a wide berth: corporeal and incorporeal entities count, whether they be material objects, abstractions, objects of intention, or anything else whatsoever—quarks, Harry Potter, keynote speeches, single-malt scotch, Land Rovers, lychee fruit, love affairs, dereferenced pointers, Mike "The Situation" Sorrentino, bozons, horticulturists, Mozambique, *Super Mario Bros.*, not one is "more real" than any other.

Bryant offers a curious and counterintuitive phrase to get to the bottom of flat ontology: "The world," he says, "does not exist."[32] Of course, if *everything* exists as I have just claimed, then statements of nonexistence demand special attention. What does Bryant mean? That there is no ur-thing, no container, no vessel, no concept that sits above being such that it can include all aspects of it holistically and incontrovertibly: "there is no 'super-object' . . . that would gather all objects together in a harmonious unity."[33]

When then to make of "the world" or "the universe"? They are concepts human agents mobilize in an attempt to contain and explain things in a neat and tidy way. As an idea in the service of philosophy or science or fiction, the world exists no more and no less than asphalt sealcoat or appletinis. But as a regulatory force that unifies and contains all within it under, say, the laws of physics or the will of God, "the universe" provides no more truthful, unitary characterization of things than any other. It is just another being among the muskmelons and the lip balms.

In my previous work I've given the name *system operations* to the top-down organizing principles symbolized by ideas like "the world" in Bryant's sense. System operations are "totalizing structures that seek to explicate a phenomenon, behavior or state in its entirety."[34] They tend to assume that some final, holistic, definitive explanation accounts for and explains being.

In our current age, two such system operations are dominant: scientific naturalism and social relativism. The first descends from Democritus and Epicurus, if indirectly. The scientific naturalist holds that some fundamental material firmament sustains and thereby explains all that is. The particulars of this ground don't particularly matter— particle physics, genetics, brain chemistry, whatever. Never mind the *sort* of stuff, for the scientific naturalist there is always *some* stuff out of which all others can be explained. Furthermore, the nature of these fundamental objects and their role in founding the world can always be discovered, documented, and solidified through the scientific process. Kuhnian paradigm shifts notwithstanding, scientific naturalism assumes the ever-progressing if incremental discovery of reality through scientific persistence.

The second ontological system operation of our time, social relativism, descends from the humanistic and social scientific traditions. For the social relativist, nothing exists that cannot be explained through the machinations of human society, particularly the complex, evolutionary forms of culture and language. The social relativist argues that all things exist through conceptualization; they are really just structures within the temple of human cultural production. For the social relativist, the certainty of the scientific naturalist is always compromised by the fact that science itself is situated within culture—and not just culture writ large but some specific cultural moment, existing at a particular time and in a particular place and making particular assumptions.

Scientific naturalism and social relativism have a long history of intellectual conflict. The distance between the disciplines that C. P. Snow famously called the "two cultures problem" suggests an irreconcilable conflict between these two positions—the former holding on to the Enlightenment ideal of true knowledge independent of history or context, the latter wagging its finger at the dangers of singular explanations that ignore the contingencies of those histories and contexts.[35]

It doesn't take much squinting to see that both positions are really cut from the same cloth. For the scientific naturalist, the world exists for human discovery and exploitation. And for the cultural relativist, humans create and refashion the world. That the two sides have so long argued about how to approach worldly knowledge—either experimentation or criticism—has only shrouded the real problem.

To wit: both perspectives embody the correlationist conceit. The scientist believes in reality apart from human life, but it is a reality excavated for human exploitation. The scientific process cares less for reality itself than it does for the discoverability of reality through human ingenuity. Likewise, the humanist doesn't believe in the world *except* as a structure erected in the interest of human culture. Like a mirror image of the scientist, the humanist mostly seeks to mine particular forms of culture, often by suggesting aspects of it that must be overcome through abstract notions of resistance or revolution. "Look at me!" shout both the scientist and the humanist. "Look what I have uncovered!"

Consider once again the computer as a case in point. Let's choose a famous example: the "Turing Test," a challenge posed in 1950 by one of the most important logicians, cryptographers, and computer architects of the twentieth century, Alan Turing.[36] His famous article "Computing Machinery and Intelligence" begins with a question that has animated the field of artificial intelligence for the six decades since: "Can machines think?" We could well stop at this first sentence, for already it contains the singular human–world correlate. Without even knowing what the details of the challenge will be, the goal is assumed: to relate machine behavior to human behavior, such that the one can be judged successful in terms of the other.

But Turing quickly explains that this question is unsatisfactory, and he plans to replace it with a different one. His eponymous test (so named by others later) turns out to be a variant of a common parlor game, in which an interlocutor attempts to guess the gender of two hidden guests at a party by posing simple questions like, "Will X please tell me the length of his or her hair?"[37] Being human, the players can try to outwit one another in order to fool the interlocutor through deception. Turing suggests replacing one of the two hidden human players with a computer. If the computer can fool the human player as often as the human, then the result satisfactorily replaces the original question, "Can machines think?"

Silly though this gambit may seem, it has long served as a holy grail for computer science and engineering. A machine, after all, is a dumb, insentient object, useful only when animated by a human operator or programmer to solve tasks—tasks meant to benefit human society, of course. The field of artificial intelligence, which emerged a few short years after Turing's proposal and untimely death, pledges fealty to the human correlate in its very name: a computer is to be considered useful the more it does *intelligent* things, that is, things that benefit human beings or things that human beings can recognize as intelligent activities. The Turing Test itself has served as both science fictional and scientific goal, whether in the form of the *Star Trek* LCARS, which can understand, reason, and relate to humans through language, or by inspiring the Loebner Prize, a competition held annually since 1991 that enacts the letter of Turing's challenge and awards prizes to its best performers. Science assumes that the nature of the computer is related to the nature of human experience. To discover the true nature of computation is also to discover the true nature of human reason.

Among the objections to the Turing Test, most reflect on the fundamental principles of human understanding and experience. The most famous such objection is John Searle's "Chinese Room" thought experiment.[38] Searle imagines a man operating as if he were a machine that manipulates Chinese characters slid under a door. While the man has no knowledge of the Chinese language, he is able to create coherent replies by following the program's instructions. Even if the resulting replies are comprehensible among native Chinese speakers, Searle argues that the machine that would execute them cannot be said to "think" or to have a "mind" or to possess "intelligence."

In a somewhat different critique, Turing's biographer Andrew Hodges suggests that Turing's personality made him predisposed to treat the world as a puzzle to be solved, but that he was tragically "blind to the distinction between saying and doing."[39] Hodges turns Turing's interest in machine intelligence into a thoughtful insight into his troubled personal life as an individual—troubles that included his persecution for being a homosexual in the 1950s and subsequent suicide. Says Hodges, "Questions involving sex, society, politics or secrets would demonstrate how what it was possible for people to say might be limited not by puzzle-solving intelligence but by the restrictions on what might be done."[40]

Searle's objection critiques the functionalism of "strong AI" for misconstruing the nature of the human mind and for misunderstanding the difference between having a mind and simulating one. Hodges's objection looks at the motivations that inspired the computational system rather than the system itself, concluding that the very idea of the Turing Test (and by extension the concept of intelligent machines) represents but a particular human's curious take on a general problem.

In both cases, the idea of computation is inextricably linked to human understanding, experience, and knowledge. Such an approach is not unreasonable: humans primarily create and manipulate machines to solve the problems that concern them. But even in the simple case of the Turing Test, the myriad other factors at work in a computer are ignored. The operation of a machine independent of its ability to model or strive for human intelligence, for example, is not a consideration for either scientific or humanistic critiques of computation. The construction and behavior of a computer system might interest engineers who wish to optimize or improve it, but rarely for the sake of *understanding* the machine itself, as if it were a buttercup or a soufflé. Yet, like everything, the computer possesses its own unique existence worthy of reflection and awe, and it's indeed capable of more than the purposes for which we animate it.

The rejection of correlationism upsets the singular human–world correlate that underwrites both humanism and science, as exemplified by Turing's computer experiment. But to oppose this human–world correlate *does not* mean rejecting human beings or their place in the world. Posthumanism has signified "human enhancement" for too long—whether through technologies of replacement or addendum or through newer, more pliant cultural understandings of human identity. A true posthumanism would neither extend humanity into a symbiotic, visionary future nor reject our place in the world via antihuman nihilism. Instead, as Bryant puts it, a posthumanist ontology is one in which "humans are no longer monarchs of being, but are instead *among* beings, *entangled* in beings, and *implicated* in other beings."[41]

Bryant has suggested that flat ontology can unite the two worlds, synthesizing the human and the nonhuman into a common collective.[42] An ontology is flat if it makes no distinction between the types of things that exist but treats all equally, the spirit behind the name Bryant gives his OOO theory, "the democracy of objects." In a flat ontology, the bubbling skin of the capsaicin pepper holds just as much interest as the culinary history of the enchilada it is destined to top.

Turing in mind, how might one flatly ontologize the computer? It cannot be done in a general sense, by broad-based definitions of computation grounded in symbolic logic or even by abstractions, such as the universal Turing Machine. Instead, a flat ontology of computation (or anything else) must be *specific* and *open-ended,* so as to make it less likely to fall into the trap of system operational overdetermination. I'll pick an example of special interest to me: the ill-fated 1982 videogame adaptation of *E.T.: The Extra-Terrestrial* for the Atari Video Computer System (VCS). What is *E.T.?* Flat ontology demands that the answers be multitudinous:

> *E.T.* is 8 kilobytes of 6502 opcodes and operands, which can be viewed by human beings as a hex dump of the ROM. Each value corresponds with a processor operation, some of which also take operands. For example, hex $69 is the opcode for adding a value.
>
> An assembled ROM is really just a reformatted version of the game's assembly code, and *E.T.* is also its source code, a series of human-legible (or slightly more human legible, anyway) mnemonics for the machine opcodes that run the game. For example, the source code uses the mnemonic "ADC" in place of the hex value $69.
>
> *E.T.* is a flow of RF modulations that result from user input and program flow altering the data in memory-mapped registers on a custom graphics and sound chip called the television interface adapter (TIA). The TIA transforms data into radio

frequencies, which it sends to the television's cathode ray tube and speakers.

E.T. is a mask ROM, a type of integrated circuit, on which memory is hardwired into an etched wafer. The photomask for a ROM of this sort is expensive to create but very cheap to manufacture in quantity.

E.T. is a molded plastic cartridge held together with a screw, covered with an adhesive, offset-printed label. It houses the mask ROM, which is flanked by a lever and a spring that reveals the chip's contacts when actuated by an Atari VCS console.

E.T. is a consumer good, a product packaged in a box and sold at retail with a printed manual and packing cardboard, hung on a hook or placed on a shelf.

E.T. is a system of rules or mechanics that produce a certain experience, one that corresponds loosely to a story about a fictional alien botanist stranded on earth, whom a group of children attempt to protect from the xenophobic curiosity of governmental and scientific violence.

E.T. is an interactive experience players can partake of individually or together when gathered around the television.

E.T. is a unit of intellectual property that can be owned, protected, licensed, sold, and violated.

E.T. is a collectible, an out of print or "scarce" object that can be bartered or displayed.

E.T. is a sign that depicts the circumstances surrounding the videogame crash of 1983, a market collapse partly blamed on low-quality shovelware (of which E.T. is often cited as a primary example). In this sense, the sign "E.T." is not just a fictional alien botanist but a notion of extreme failure, of "the worst game of all time": the famed dump of games in the Alamogordo landfill, the complex culture of greed and design constraint that led to it, the oversimplified scapegoating process that ensued thereafter—otherwise put, "E.T." is Atari's "Waterloo."

All of these sorts of being exist simultaneously with, yet independently from, one another. There is no one "real" E.T., be it the structure, characterization, and events of a narrative, or the code that produces it, or the assemblage of cartridge-machine-player-market, or anything in between. Latour calls it irreduction: "Nothing can be reduced to anything else," even if certain aspects of a thing could be considered transformative on something else.

Latour describes transformation in terms of networks of human or nonhuman actors behaving on one another, entering and exiting relation. My notion of the unit operation, to which I return below, offers another model—a unit being made up of a set of other units (again human or nonhuman), irrespective of scale. Moves like these allow us to steer between the Scylla of cultural relativism, a common critique of media studies and social scientific analyses of subjects like computing, and the Charybdis of scientific reductionism, a common problem with formal and material analyses of those subjects. *E.T.* is never only one of the things just mentioned, nor is it only a collection of all of these things. Paradoxically, a flat ontology allows it to be both and neither. We can distinguish the ontological status of computer program-as-code from game-as-play-session without making appeal to an ideal notion of game as form, type, or transcendental. The power of flat ontology comes from its indiscretion. It refuses distinction and welcomes all into the temple of being.

TINY ONTOLOGY

Flat ontology is an ideal, a value that a wide variety of metaphysical positions could adopt. I embrace the principle, but I also wish to extend it even farther. Being is various and unitary all at once. How might we characterize it?

I appreciate Latour's answer, which seats all things within networks of relation. Yet problems arise: for one, being seems to owe too much to relation for Latour, whereby interactions sit outside rather than within the being of a thing. For another, the "network" is an overly normalized structure, one driven by order and predefinition. A generous effort to retain Latourian actor-network theory might replace *network* with Latour's later notion of the *imbroglio*, a confusion in which "it's never clear who and what is acting."[43] His original example of the imbroglio is unfortunately bound to human knowledge, such as the way reading a newspaper involves us in a tangle of different fields and areas, connected but hybridized. (Says

Latour, "Hybrid [newspaper] articles sketch out imbroglios of science, politics, economy, law, religion, technology, fiction. . . . All of culture and all of nature get churned up again every day, . . . yet no one seems to find this troubling.")[44] But the imbroglio still feels too formal, too organized for my taste. An imbroglio is an intellectual kind of predicament, a muddle to be sure, but a muddle wearing a monocle.

Perhaps instead we could adopt actor-network theorist John Law's take on the same problem. Law tells a story about a research project he helped conduct that investigated a hospital trust's management of patients with alcohol-caused liver diseases.[45] As in many bureaucratic situations, they quickly discovered considerable logistical complexity. In some cases, but not others, patients from a city-central advice center were advised to go to treatment programs, but they'd have to make an appointment. Yet many in the hospital didn't have the same perception of the advice center, considering it a location for drop-in treatment. The situation was, Law concluded pragmatically, a "mess."

Law promotes *mess* to a methodological concept, one that resists creating neat little piles of coherent analysis. Instead, it's necessary to pursue "non-coherence." Says Law, "This is the problem of talking about 'mess': it is a put-down used by those who are obsessed with making things tidy. My preference, rather, is to relax the border controls, allow the non-coherences to make themselves manifest. Or rather, it is to start to think about ways in which we might go about this."[46]

Note the difference between Law's mess and the formalism of structuralist approaches: it is not some overarching system operation that accounts for all things, a set of cultural mores, or a list of regulations for a particularly well-scheduled orgy to be held on glossy birch flooring, but a loose-and-fast structuring of things-for-whatever, not just for the human actors implicated in events.

A mess is not a pile, which is neatly organized even if situated in an inconvenient place underfoot. A mess is not an elegant thing of a higher order. It is not an intellectual project to be evaluated and risk-managed by waistcoat-clad underwriters. A mess is a strew of inconvenient and sometimes repellent things. A mess is an accident.

A mess is a thing that you find where you don't want it. We recoil at it, yet there it is, and we must deal with it.

Yet for all its aesthetic appeal, I find the mess wanting as much as the imbroglio. If the network is too orderly, the mess is too disorderly. Like flat ontology, it spreads things out in order to draw them in. It posits a lurid if intractable picture of the massive dispersion of beings, but then it provides no common ground that unites them. Furthermore, even if just by metaphor, the mess bears a correlationist taint: a mess is what is not graspable by *human* actors, unable to be ordered into a network. But who's to say that my mess is not the volcano's network? Whose conception of reality gets to frame that of everything else's?

Indeed, the problem of correlationism could be restated as the problem of external reality. Science functions like a spacecraft, its brilliant and insane voyagers looking out fancy windscreens, eager to discover and map the world without. Humanism and social science function in reverse, their clever time travelers doubling back to demonstrate that the outside world was always already inside in the first place, only delusion and naïveté making it appear to be separate. In both cases, a metaphor of three-dimensionality describes the palace of being: either it is a structure that can be explored and mapped for the benefit of human culture, like a great cathedral, or it is the shape that encloses that structure, giving it form in the way that a plot of land makes possible the erection of the cathedral in the first place.

Theories of being tend to be grandiose, but they need not be, because being is simple. Simple enough that it could be rendered via screen print on a trucker's cap. I call it *tiny ontology*, precisely because it ought not demand a treatise or a tome. I don't mean that the domain of being is small—quite the opposite, as I'll soon explain. Rather, the basic ontological apparatus needed to describe existence ought to be as compact and unornamented as possible.

An alternative metaphor to the two-dimensional plane of flat ontology is that of spacelessness, of one-dimensionality. If any one being exists no less than any other, then instead of scattering such beings all across the two-dimensional surface of flat ontology, we might also collapse them into the infinite density of a dot. Instead of the *plane* of flat ontology, I suggest the *point* of tiny ontology. It's a dense mass of everything contained entirely—even as it's spread about haphazardly like a mess or organized logically like a network.

In the customary account of general relativity, a black hole is a singularity, a point where matter reaches infinite density. But the physicist Nikodem Popławski has argued that the gravitation of such enormous mass reverses, causing matter to expand once more.[47] Popławski suggests that black holes might thus contain entire universes—we may even be living in one. We can never know, because even if one could approach a black hole, time would slow down for the observer because of gravitational time dilation. Speculation is thus required to consider the implications of being within a singularity.

As it happens, Harman also compares the thing itself to the black hole. Every object, says Harman, "is not only protected by a vacuous shield from the things that lie outside it, but also harbors and nurses an erupting infernal universe within."[48] Flat ontology suggests that there is no hierarchy of being, and we must thus conclude that *being itself* is an object no different from any other. The withdrawal of being is not merely a feature of yogurt or tonsils or Winnie the Pooh, but also of its very self. The embroiderable shorthand for tiny ontology might read simply, *is*, but only because semantic coherence cannot be contained in the tittle atop the *i* alone.

UNIT OPERATIONS

On the one side of being, we find unfathomable density, the black hole outside which all distinctions collapse into indistinction. Yet, on the other side, we find that being once again expands into an entire universe worth of stuff. Thanks to the structure of tiny ontology, this relationship is fractal—infinite and self-similar. The container ship is a unit as much as the cargo holds, the shipping containers, the hydraulic rams, the ballast water, the twist locks, the lashing rods, the crew, their sweaters, and the yarn out of which those garments are knit. The ship erects a boundary in which everything it contains withdraws within it, while those individual units that compose it do so similarly, simultaneously, and at the same fundamental level of existence. This strange mereology, to use Levi Bryant's phrase for it, underscores the weird relationship between parts and wholes.

For OOO, "one object is simultaneously a part of another object *and* an independent object in its own right."[49] Things are independent from their constituent parts while remaining dependent on them.

An object is thus a weird structure that might refer to a "normal," middle-sized object such as a toaster as much as it might describe an enormous, amorphous object like global transport logistics. As Tim Morton quips, "An object is like Doctor Who's Tardis, bigger on the inside than it is on the outside."[50] Things are both ordinary and strange, both large and small, both concrete and abstract. We need a way to characterize them effectively.

In the past, I have suggested the term *unit* as a synonym for and alternative to *object* or *thing*.[51] Part of my rationale was purely pragmatic: I write about computation, and in computer science the terms *object* and *object-oriented* bear a specific meaning, one related to a particular paradigm of computer programming. When Harman suggests the term *object-oriented philosophy* to name a set of positions that refuse to privilege the human–world relationship as the only one, he borrows this phrase from the computational world and gives it new life in philosophy.[52] I have no objections to the repurposing of terms, but in the context of discussions of the particular objects in my area of interest, *object* sometimes introduces confusion.

There are other reasons to avoid the term. For one, an *object* implies a *subject*, and the marriage of subject and object sits at the heart of correlationism. In truth, nothing about OOO is incompatible with the notion of a subject; the problem lies in the assumption that only *one* subject—the human subject—is of interest or import. There's good rhetorical reason to steer clear of this problem by avoiding the term *object* in the first place.

For another, *object* implies materiality, physical stuff, like cinderblocks and bendy straws and iron filings. Object-oriented realisms are indeed concerned with recovering the world's lost material and returning it to the center of philosophical inquiry, but material things *alone* do not sufficiently exemplify that concern. To invoke the principle of tiny ontology, the objects of object-oriented thought mean to encompass *anything whatsoever,* from physical matter (a Slurpee frozen beverage) to properties (frozenness) to marketplaces (the convenience store industry) to symbols (the Slurpee brand name) to ideas (a best guess about where to find a 7-11). The density of being makes it *promiscuous*, always touching everything else, unconcerned with differentiation. Anything is thing enough to party.

Speaking of which, *thing* offers itself as an alternative to *object*. Unlike objects, things can be concrete or abstract. But "thing" has a charged philosophical history, too. Kant's *thing-in-itself* (*das Ding an Sich*) is the unknowable element that must be inferred through experience. For Heidegger, a thing is a human-created object, one with particular functions. *Das Ding*, he argues in a characteristic etymological analysis, originally meant a gathering or assemblage. Heidegger interprets this gathering as a convocation of human and world. An *object* becomes a *thing* for Heidegger when it stands out against the backdrop of existence in use—human use, of course. For Sigmund Freud the Thing is a lost object, what's absent in the subject. Jacques Lacan translates Freud's neuronal understanding of the Thing into a semiotic one; the Thing is the signifier cut off from the chain of signification, which Lacan later calls *objet a*. Harman uses the words interchangeably ("objects, tool-beings, substances or things"), but *object* remains his preferred term—perhaps in partial response to the troubled philosophical history of *thing*.[53]

There have been other extensions of *thing* into critical theory, most notably Bill Brown's proposal of "thing theory" as an analogue to narrative theory or cultural theory.[54] Brown is on to something (he invokes Francis Ponge, that great modernist poet of fire, rain, oranges, and cigarettes), but, as for Heidegger before him, the critic's interest in things remains motivated by human concerns: it turns out Brown intends thing theory to help us understand "how inanimate objects constitute human subjects."[55] On the one hand, *thing* offers a helpful way to shroud the object, reminding us of its withdrawal from others. But on the other hand, the subject of that withdrawal has so frequently been *us* that a reliance on *thing* carries considerable baggage.

One last border problem plagues *things*: concreteness. When the skin of the capsaicin pepper bubbles and chafes against the hot steel grating of the rotating roaster, its encounter with its vessel is both undeniably close and familiar, yet simultaneously distant and alien. As the human vendor rotates the drum or sets it nearby on the turned-down tailgate of a red pickup truck, the drum, handle, tailgate, asphalt, pepper, metal, and propane all distance themselves from him and from one another. But another sort of thing also distances in this situation: the relations between those other objects themselves, that between pepper and iron, tailgate and Levi's 501s, asphalt and pickup. It's not just things that are objects but abstractions of and relations between them as well.[56] It happens fast and hot, the tiny universes of things bumping and rubbing against one another in succession, chaining together like polymers.

Thing, then, is too eager to pin things down to satisfy tiny ontology. A thing is not just a thing for humans, but a thing for many other things as well, both material and immaterial. Yet a thing remains unitary even as it finds itself altering and coalescing into the myriad configurations of different moments within being.

This is why *unit* becomes helpful as a name for objects or things. It is an ambivalent term, indifferent to the nature of what it names. It is also isolated, unitary, and specific, not simply the part of a whole or ontologically basic and indivisible like an atom. As I have argued elsewhere, "unit" finds precedent in systems theory and complexity theory, including applications in biology, cybernetics, chemical engineering, computer science, social theory, and the myriad other domains that seek to explain phenomena as the emergent effects of the autonomous actions of interrelating parts of a system.[57] Counterintuitively, a system and a unit represent three things at once: for one, a unit is isolated and unique. For another, a unit encloses a system—an entire universe's worth. For yet another, a unit becomes part of another system—often many other systems— as it jostles about.

These systems of units are held together tenuously by accidents. I have adapted the word *operation* to describe how units behave and interact. In systems theory, an operation is "a basic process that takes one or more inputs and performs a transformation on it."[58] Any sort of function can be understood as an operation: brewing tea, shedding skin, photosynthesizing sugar, igniting compressed fuel. In the past, I've used the phrase *unit operation* primarily as a method to describe semiotic systems—particularly the unique properties of computational signification, since such expression always relies on procedural behavior.[59] But, philosophically speaking, the unit operation is a much more general concept, one sufficient to describe any system whatsoever. Indeed, just as Harman repurposes "object-oriented" from computing, I have absconded with "unit operation" from chemical engineering, a field in which the name refers to the steps in a process (extraction, homogenization, distillation, refrigeration, etc.).

The unit reveals a feature of being that the thing and the object occlude. The density and condensation of tiny ontology has a flip side: something is always something else, too: a gear in another mechanism, a relation in another assembly, a part in another whole. Within the black hole–like density of being, things undergo an expansion. The ontological equivalent of the Big Bang rests within every object. Being expands.

In my original theory of unit operations, I describe this expansion philosophically by means of Alain Badiou's set theoretical ontology.[60] Badiou adopts Georg Cantor's concept of the set, a way to describe a totality by enumerating its members, like this: {a,b,c}. A subset of any set, {a,b} or {b,c}, contains some smaller number of the set's total members. Cantor built a theory of *transfinity* by representing infinity as sets: an infinite set is one that corresponds to the set of all natural numbers. But the set of all possible subsets of an infinite set seems to be a "larger" infinity.

Badiou builds his ontology around Cantor's insight about transfinite numbers. For Badiou, being is membership: "To exist is to be an element *of*."[61] For membership to make ontological sense, some process must exist to isolate beings from the transfinite subsets available, to "one-ify" them, in Peter Hallward's words.[62] Badiou names this process of concocting a new multiplicity the *count-as-one* (*compte-pour-un*). And he gives the name *situation* to the output of this gesture, "a set configured in a particular way."[63]

Badiou's mathematical jargon notwithstanding, *configuration* can help us understand tiny ontology. If everything exists all at once and equally, with no differentiation whatsoever, then the processes by which units perceive, relate, consider, respond, retract, and otherwise engage with one another—the method by which the unit operation takes place—is a configurative one. In that respect, the Badiouian count-as-one offers a helpful analogy for how the black hole density on the one side of being expands into infinite arrangements on the other side. The stuff of being constantly shuffles and rearranges itself, reorienting physically and metaphysically as it jostles up against material, relations, and concepts.

Think of it this way: the set offers an exploded view onto being. On the flip side of a unit's density, it expands like the universe contained in the black hole. That expansion gets cataloged in the set, a structured account of the unit's constituents akin to a poster that calls out the many mechanisms of a large machine like a container ship or a jumbo jet.

There's a problem with Badiou's ontology, however, which prevents me from adopting it wholesale: who does the counting? Badiou leaves the answer ambiguous, equating being with the structureless impersonality of mathematics.[64] But this is an unsatisfactory response, since the aloofness of being in philosophical history is almost always shrugged off by a transcendental agent or by humans themselves. Given that set theory is a human-derived, symbolic abstraction for the concept of membership (even if it aspires toward universality), and given that Badiou's own examples of the count-as-one are almost entirely those of human experience (politics, art, love, poetry), retaining the count-as-one as a move for units is impossible.

Instead, consider this simple declaration: *units operate*. That is, things constantly machinate within themselves and mesh with one another, acting and reacting to properties and states while still keeping something secret. Alphonso Lingis calls these behaviors the imperatives that structure the perception of things: "The *inner ordinance* which makes the grapefruit coagulate with its rubbery rind, its dense dull yellow, its loose inner pulp" or the "*inner formula* of a mango, a willow tree, or a flat smooth stone."[65] These inner ordinances or formulas of things withdraw; they are not grasped, even if they order perception like an imperative.

The scale of such operation is varied: the cell feeds and divides to repopulate the organ that circulates blood to the limb of the body that lifts the burrito. The revolving feeder of the combine harvester gathers cereal crops and pushes them across the vehicle's cutter, to the augers that carry them up to the machine's threshing drum. The philology of the fictional Languages of Arda forms the basis of the history and lore of Middle Earth, which J. R. R. Tolkien documents in the literary works *The Hobbit, The Lord of the Rings*, and *The Silmarillion*, which in turn ground fan-created interpretations of those worlds. In all of these cases, units partake of one another, engaging through various acts and gestures, material and immaterial, as they coalesce together and recede again.

If we hold on to Badiou's mathematical metaphor, the members of a set describe their configuration but not their behavior. We might adopt Badiou's notion of the "event" to characterize the doing of things, but for Badiou events are not commonplace affairs. Rather, they are wholesale changes (this is another reason to believe that sets are configurable only by humans). The simplest acts of set members remain unaccounted for. When seen in this light, it's clear that the count-as-one doesn't deal with the mundane interactions of set members in the first place. Badiou's ontology appears incapable of describing the ordinary being of things, limiting itself to the extraordinary being of human change.

In *Unit Operations*, I offer the count-as-one not as a model for or analogue to the unit operation but as a related idea.[66] The point is this: things are not *merely* what they do, but things *do indeed do things*. And the *way things do* is worthy of philosophical consideration. Units are isolated entities trapped together inside other units, rubbing shoulders with one another uncomfortably while never overlapping. A unit is never an atom, but a set, a grouping of other units that act together as a system; the unit operation is always fractal. These things *wonder* about one another without getting confirmation. This is the heart of the unit operation: it names a phenomenon of accounting for an object. It is a process, a logic, an algorithm if you want, by which a unit attempts to make sense of another. In Badiou's terms, it is the sense of a situation rather than the counting-for-one that establishes it. In Whitehead's terms, it is a prehensive capability. In Husserl's terms, it is *noesis* divorced of consciousness, cogitation, intention, and other accidents of human reasoning. In Lingis's terms, it is the inner formula by which a thing invites its exploration. Since objects are all fundamentally different from one another, each one has its own approach, its own logic of sense making, and through this relation they trace the real reality of another, just as the radiation around an event horizon helps an astronomer deduce the nature of a black hole.[67] "Unit operation" names the logics by which objects perceive and engage their worlds.

SPECULATION

I am seduced by the speculative realist rebuff of the human–world correlate. Yet questions remain: even if we accept the rejection of correlationism as overtly, selfishly anthropocentric, how do we deal with things that are also complex structures or systems crafted or used by humans? And even more so, how do we as humans strive to understand the relationships between *particular* objects in the world, relations that go on without us, even if we may be their cause, subject, or beneficiary? How do we understand the green chile or the integrated circuit both as things left to themselves and as things interacting with others, us among them?

Harman's answer goes like this: the idea we have of things really is present, but the things themselves still withdraw infinitely. Meillassoux's is somewhat different: things are mathematically thinkable even if not sensible.[68] These responses are difficult to muster in practice. But what else would one expect when consorting with metaphysicians? Despite their luridness, speculative realisms remain philosophies of first principles. They have not yet concerned themselves with particular implementations, although they are also not incompatible with them. Yet if its goal is to make redress against Kant's Copernican Revolution, speculative realism would benefit from an extension beyond first principles, into the *practice* of metaphysics itself.

Perhaps the theory I seek is a *pragmatic speculative realism*, not in the Jamesian sense but more softly: an applied speculative realism, an object-oriented engineering to ontology's physics. Such a method would embolden the actual philosophical treatment of actual material objects and their relations. If we take speculativism seriously, then why might philosophy not muster the same concrete grounding as, say, speculative fiction or magical realism?[69] The science fiction author Robert A. Heinlein advocates speculating about possible worlds that are unlike our own, but in a way that remains coupled to the actual world more than the term *science fiction* might normally suggest. Likewise, the magical realism of Gabriel García Márquez or Isabel Allende suggests that the spectacular is real insofar as it actually comprises aspects of culture. In cases like these, the philosopher's tendency to abstract takes a backseat to the novelist's tendency to specify. The result is something particular whose branches bristle into the canopy of the conceptual.

Only some portion of the domain of being is obvious to any given object at a particular time. For the udon noodle, the being of the soup bowl does not intersect with the commercial transaction through which the noodle house sells it, or the social conventions according to which the eater slurps it. Yet there is no reason to believe that the entanglement in which the noodle finds itself is any less complex than the human who shapes, boils, vends, consumes, or digests it.

When we ask *what it means to be something,* we pose a question that exceeds our own grasp of the being of the world. These unknown unknowns characterize things about an object that may or may not be obvious—or even knowable. The accusations of "naive realism" that sometimes accompany such a position—claims that the world is just how we perceive of or know it—manage little reproach, for the problem of the being of the udon noodle or the nuclear warhead consists precisely in the ways those objects *exceed* what we know or ever can know about them.

That things are is not a matter of debate. *What it means that something in particular is for another thing that is*: this is the question that interests me. The significance of one thing to another differs depending on the perspectives of both. Since units remain fundamentally in the dark about one another's infinite centers, the unit operations that become relevant to them differ. A unit's means of making sense of another is not universal and cannot be explained away through natural law, scientific truth, or even its own perspective. The unit operation entails deductions in the light of impossible verification—units never take one another as they are but only as a kind of burlesque. To perform philosophical work on unit operations is a practice of speculation.

In philosophy, "speculation" has a particular meaning that must be overcome. Traditionally, speculative philosophy names metaphysical claims that cannot be verified through experience or through science. It is here that the loosey-goosey abstractions of scruffy-bearded, sandal-wearing philosophy takes root, in questions like *What is being?* or *What is thought?* Speculative philosophy is sometimes contrasted with critical philosophy, which involves the testing and verification of theories.

But another kind of speculative philosophy exists, too, one that describes the nature of being rather than the human philosopher's approach to it. Speculative realism names not only speculative philosophy that takes existence to be separate from thought but also a philosophy *claiming that things speculate* and, furthermore, one *that speculates about how things speculate.*

A *speculum* is a mirror, but not in the modern sense of the term as a device that reflects back the world as it really is, unimpeded and undistorted. As Narcissus proved, a reflection is different enough to hold power, including the power of drunk love. The lesson holds beyond mythology: from ancient times through the middle ages, a mirror was an imprecise device, usually a convex disc of polished metal that reflected enough light to give a viewer a rough sense of the figure placed in front of it. Only a rough sense: a representation, an imitation, a *caricature,* to use Harman's word for it. The speculum of speculation is not a thin, flat plate of glass onto which a layer of molten aluminum has been vacuum-sprayed but a funhouse mirror made of hammered metal, whose distortions show us a perversion of a unit's sensibilities.

In the face of such wackiness, one must proceed like the carnival barker rather than the scholar: through educated guesswork. Speculation isn't just poetic, but it's partly so, a creative act that beings conduct as they gaze earnestly but bemusedly at one another. Everything whatsoever is like people on a subway, crunched together into uncomfortably intimate contact with strangers.

The philosopher's job is not merely that of *documenting the state* of this situation but of *making an effort to grapple with it* in particular circumstances. Here we might think of Heidegger's distinction between thinking scientifically and thinking ontologically, but such a notion goes only so far, as it's limited to human thought and action—

it doesn't make much sense to ponder the ontotheology of noodle bowls or of combine harvesters.

If unit operations characterize the logics of objects, then they fall under the purview of phenomenology, the area of metaphysics concerned with how stuff appears to beings. Unlike Heidegger, Edmund Husserl theorizes sensation as a general principle, although he casts it in a human-centered fashion by naming it "consciousness." Still, Husserl's consciousness is a process that remains abstracted from the material accidents of brains or microprocessors or combustion engines or unleavened dough.[70] The means by which consciousness (or whatever term might replace it) grasps objects is *itself* a subject of speculation. That is, when we consider the encounter between two units, the givenness or appearance of reality for each of them *is not given to us*. In Lingis's terms, the mango's inner formula is never grasped.[71]

For Husserl, in order to consider appearances seriously we must avoid commonsensical presuppositions. We cannot escape the attitude we portray toward the world, but we must *bracket* its validity. Husserl gives the name *epoché* (ἐποχή, suspension) to this procedure of bracketing our natural assumptions about perception. As Dan Zahavi explains, the epoché "entails a change of attitude toward reality, and not an exclusion of reality."[72]

The speculation required to consider the unit operations that entangle beings requires something similar to Husserl's phenomenal act. Speculation is akin to epoché. It produces *transcendence* in the Husserlian sense: a concrete and individual notion, one that grips the fiery-hot, infinitely dense molten core of an object and projects it outside, where it becomes its own unit, a new and creative unit operation for a particular set of interactions. It's a phenomenology, to be sure. But it's a phenomenology that explodes like shrapnel, leaving behind the human as solitary consciousness like the Voyager spacecraft leaves behind the heliosphere on its way beyond the boundaries of the solar system.

ALIEN PHENOMENOLOGY

Harman uses the name "black noise" to describe the background noise of peripheral objects: "It is not a white noise of screeching, chaotic qualities demanding to be shaped by the human mind, but rather a black noise of muffled objects hovering at the fringes of our attention."[73] *Black* is the color of sonic noise that approaches silence, allowing emissions of but a few spikes of energy. Similarly, in physics a black body is an object that absorbs all the electromagnetic radiation it encounters, emitting a spectrum of light commensurate with its temperature. This *blackbody radiation* can be seen on the visible spectrum, from red to white as it increases in temperature. Among other applications, blackbody radiation can be used to evaluate the nature of celestial bodies. In particular, a black hole can be identified through the type of blackbody radiation it discharges.

Just as the astronomer understands stars through the radiant energy that surrounds them, so the philosopher understands objects by tracing their impacts on the surrounding ether. If the black noise of objects is akin to the Hawking radiation that quantum effects deflect from black holes, then perhaps it's there, in the unknown universe, that we should ground a method.

In 2009, after a century of experiments with radio telescopes, SETI had a new revelation: if there are aliens on other worlds, they probably use Twitter. The organization's "Earth Speaks" project invited website users to answer the question, "If we discover intelligent life beyond Earth, should we reply, and if so, what should we say?"[74] By harnessing the dubious power of collective intelligence, SETI assembled possible transmissions like "Get down off your cloud and have some tequila shots. . . . We can discuss many things." The site's research statement explains, "Rather than trying to identify a unified 'Message from Earth,' the current project will help understand differing perspectives on the appropriate content of interstellar messages, drawing on the PI's Dialogic Model for interstellar message design."[75] Earth Speaks shows how time has not altered SETI's fundamental assumption: if there is life in the universe, it ought to be able to *recognize* its counterparts by pointing radio astronomy apparatuses like the VLA in their direction, and to *understand* their answer.

In the 1980s the prolific German American philosopher Nicholas Rescher argued against SETI's insistence that the signs of extraterrestrial life would resemble detectable communication technology. Extraterrestrials, Rescher suggested, are perhaps so alien that their science and technology is incomprehensible to us; we could never understand it as intelligence.[76] I'll push Rescher's idea even farther: it's not just that the communications technologies of the alien escape our comprehension, but that their very idea of "life" might not correspond with ours. The alien might not be life, at all. As Bernhard Waldenfels puts it, the alien is "the inaccessibility of a particular region of experience and sense."[77] Still, Waldenfels follows Husserl in characterizing experience of the alien (*Fremderfahrung*) as a process of intersubjectivity—the experience of other people. But the alien is not limited to another *person*, or even another *creature*. The alien is anything—and everything—to everything else.

The true alien recedes interminably even as it surrounds us completely. It is not hidden in the darkness of the outer cosmos or in the deep-sea shelf but in plain sight, everywhere, in everything. Mountain summits and gypsum beds, chile roasters and buckshot, microprocessors and ROM chips can no more communicate with us and one another than can Rescher's extraterrestrial. It is an instructive and humbling sign. Speculative realism really does *require* speculation: benighted meandering in an exotic world of utterly incomprehensible objects. As philosophers, our job is to amplify the black noise of objects to make the resonant frequencies of the stuffs inside them hum in credibly satisfying ways. Our job is to write the speculative fictions of their processes, of their unit operations. Our job is to get our hands dirty with grease, juice, gunpowder, and gypsum. Our job is to go where *everyone* has gone before, but where few have bothered to linger.

I call this practice *alien phenomenology*.

[2]

ONTOGRAPHY

Revealing the Rich Variety of Being

King Aethelberht II, the ruler of East Anglia, was executed by Offa of Mercia in 794. There was a time when many held the opinion that Offa led an early unification of England, and indeed Offa did contribute to the expansion of Mercia from the Trent River valley to much of the area now known as the English Midlands. More recently, Offa's invasions have been explained in more straightforward terms: as megalomania and bloodlust. Given this context, Aethelberht's later canonization was justified by martyrdom: he had visited the court of Offa at Sutton Walls in Herefordshire in an earnest attempt to make peace with Offa by asking for his daughter Etheldreda's hand in marriage. Offa took advantage of the situation, detaining and then beheading Aethelberht, then soon after invading and capturing East Anglia.

Montague Rhodes James is responsible for much of the definitive scholarship on St. Aethelberht, work made possible thanks to excavations he conducted at the Bury St. Edmunds Abbey in West Suffolk. Among fragments unearthed there was the twelfth-century vita of St. Aethelberht, which James reconstructed in the 1910s.

But like his countryman C. S. Lewis, James is rarely remembered for his medieval scholarship. Instead, we know him best as M. R. James, author of classic collections of ghost stories, including *Ghost Stories of an Antiquary*. Still, traces of James's medievalist roots reveal themselves like apparitions on his pages, usually in the form of gentleman–scholar protagonists who accidentally release supernatural wrath from an antique collectible.

One such tale, "Oh Whistle and I'll Come to You, My Lad," begins like this:

> "I suppose you will be getting away pretty soon, now Full Term is over, Professor," said a person not in the story to the Professor of Ontography, soon after they had sat down next to each other at a feast in the hospitable hall of St James's College.

In the story, the antique in question turns out to be an inscribed bronze whistle that, when blown by the naive Professor Parkins, summons the requisite ghost. But for our purposes, the interesting bit is not the apparition but the professor's unusual field of expertise, *ontography*.[1]

James might have intended the term to be a then contemporary absurdism, like Don DeLillo's satirical Professor of Hitler Studies in *White Noise*. Such was Graham Harman's reaction to finding the term.[2] Ontography, Harman reasoned, "would deal with a limited number of dynamics that can occur between all different sorts of objects," an initial take on what he would later develop into a full-fledged part of his philosophy. My adoption of "ontography" offers a different interpretation of this received invention than that of Harman.

As it turns out, the term is not quite an invention, although it's hardly commonplace either. In his 1988 book *The World View of Contemporary Physics*, Richard F. Kitchener declares, "Ontology is the theory of the nature of existence, and ontography is its description."[3] Kinematics, transformation theory, and relativity offer examples, ideas not so far from Harman's back-of-the-napkin sketch of Professor Parkins. Along these same lines, the science and technology studies scholar Michael Lynch suggests that "ontography is a descriptive alternative to its grand-theoretical counterpart."[4]

Other sources, if perhaps a bit untrustworthy, suggest that despite its obscurity ontography very much (and very aptly) exists. According to Susan Schulten, the geographer William Morris Davis (who was also an American contemporary of James and a professor at Harvard) deployed the term to describe "the human response to the physical landscape."[5] Schulten argues that ontography "moved geography toward a general concern with the causal relation between humans and their earth."[6] This take on ontography may be laced with too much correlationism to take root in my garden, but it does sow a promising seed.

Another, more recent application of the concept comes from Tobias Kuhn, a Swiss informaticist who has developed a method of ontography for depicting controlled natural languages (CNLs)— grammatically and semantically simplified languages for use in situations where reduced ambiguity is desirable, such as in technical documentation.[7] Kuhn's method uses a graphical notation he calls "ontographs." Each ontograph "consists of a legend that introduces types and relations and of a mini world that introduces individuals, their types, and their relations" (Figure 1).[8] A related but more familiar approach can be found in IKEA assembly instructions, which renounce language entirely in order to be more readily usable in any of the thirty-seven nations served by the company's products for the home.[9] Kitchener's, Davis's, and Kuhn's approaches have something in common: an interest in diversity and specificity.

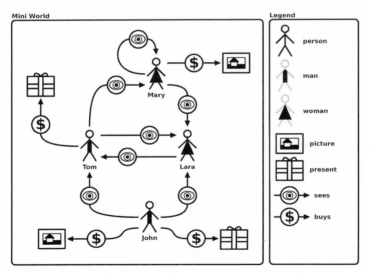

FIGURE 1. Tobias Kuhn's ontograph framework is a graphical notation for representing types and relations in controlled natural languages, a kind of formal language used in contexts where formalization or simplification are desirable, such as technical documentation.

Quentin Meillassoux uses the phrase "the great outdoors" to describe the outside reality that correlationism had stolen from philosophy.[10] The great outdoors involves both untold cosmic and worldly paraphernalia as well as the reentry into a singular existential domain, one no longer broken down into crass hemispheres of nature and culture. Both Meillassoux and Bruno Latour describe this binary as closed-minded, blinkered.[11] Once we put down the trappings of culture and take the invitation into that great outdoors, a tremendous wave of surprise and unexpectedness would overwhelm us—a "global ether" of incredible novelty and unfamiliarity.[12] As Latour sums up, "If you are mixed up with trees, how do you know they are not using you to achieve their dark designs?"[13]

Faced with such a situation, the first reaction we might have is that of the registrar, taking note of the many forms of being. Let's adopt *ontography* as a name for a general inscriptive strategy, one that uncovers the repleteness of units and their interobjectivity. From the perspective of metaphysics, ontography involves the revelation of object relationships without necessarily offering clarification or description of any kind. Like a medieval bestiary, ontography can take the form of a compendium, a record of things juxtaposed to demonstrate their overlap and imply interaction through collocation. The simplest approach to such recording is the *list*, a group of items loosely joined not by logic or power or use but by the gentle knot of the comma. Ontography is an aesthetic set theory, in which a particular configuration is celebrated merely on the basis of its existence.

Lists, as it happens, appear regularly in Latour's works. They function primarily as provocations, as litanies of surprisingly contrasted curiosities. One doesn't need to look very hard to find examples of these Latour litanies, as I call them:

A storm, a rat, a rock, a lake, a lion, a child, a worker, a gene, a slave, the unconscious, a virus.

Elections, mass demonstrations, books, miracles, viscera laid open on the altar, viscera laid out on the operating table, figures, diagrams and plans, cries, monsters, exhibitions at the pillory.

The tree that springs up again, the locusts that devour the
crops, the cancer that beats others at its own game, the mullahs who dissolve the Persian empire, the Zionists who loosen
the hold of the mullahs, the concrete in the power station
that cracks, the acrylic blues that consume other pigments,
the lion that does not follow the predictions of the oracle.[14]

Following Latour's lead, Harman also adopts the rhetoric of lists,
whether as introduction ("object-oriented philosophy holds that the
relation of humans to pollen, oxygen, eagles, or windmills is no different in kind from the interaction of these objects with each other"),[15]
as argument ("For we ourselves, just like Neanderthals, sparrows,
mushrooms, and dirt, have never done anything else than act amidst
the bustle of other actants"),[16] or as emphasis ("among the coral reefs,
sorghum fields, paragliders, ant colonies, binary stars, sea voyages,
Asian swindlers, and desolate temples").[17] He offers a defense and
justification for lists:

> Some readers may . . . dismiss them as an "incantation" or
> "poetics" of objects. But most readers will not soon grow tired,
> since the rhetorical power of these rosters of beings stems from
> their direct opposition to the flaws of current mainstream phi-
> losophy. . . . The best stylistic antidote to this grim deadlock
> is a repeated sorcerer's chant of the multitude of things that
> resist any unified empire.[18]

Litanies are not indulgences; they do indeed perform real philosophical work. Yet naming objects is only one ontographical method, the
most basic one. In addition to mere mention, things also ought to be
considered conjunctively, lest the lighthouse, dragonfly, lawnmower,
and barley all collapse into the abstraction of example without exem-
plification.

In his curious book *The Chatto Book of Cabbages and Kings*,
Francis Spufford explains why lists feel troublesome in literature:

> Language usually puts the signs that represent things into
> definite relationships with each other. Syntax joins: *I want to*

be loved by you, or *the sky is falling*, or *Mr Murdoch has bought The Times*. Lists, however, divide, or leave divided, the things they include. They offer only the relationship of accumulation: *I, you, love, sky, fall, purchase, Mr Murdoch, The Times*. Lists refuse the connecting powers of language, in favor of a sequence of disconnected elements.[19]

The inherent partition between things is a premise of OOO, and lists help underscore those separations, turning the flowing legato of a literary account into the jarring staccato of real being. Lists offer an antidote to the obsession with Deleuzean becoming, a preference for continuity and smoothness instead of sequentiality and fitfulness. The familiar refrain of "becoming-whatever" (it doesn't matter what!) suggests comfort and compatibility in relations between units, thanks to the creative negotiations things make with each other. By contrast, alien phenomenology assumes the opposite: incompatibility. The off-pitch sound of lists to the literary ear only emphasizes their real purpose: disjunction instead of flow. Lists remind us that no matter how fluidly a system may operate, its members nevertheless remain utterly isolated, mutual aliens.

Yet Spufford underestimates the ontological scope of lists. Lists do not just rebuff the connecting powers *of language* but rebuff the connecting powers of *being itself*. As he observes, "No one scribbles down a helpful sonnet before going shopping. . . . Finding a list in a book or a poem is an immediate reminder of the most obvious differences between literature and every other kind of non-performing art: literature is made out of something, language, that is an everyday stuff."[20] Philosophers, literary critics, and theorists spend so much of their time dealing with textual material that they risk forgetting about the ordinary status of such material. When made of language, lists remind the literary-obsessed that the stuff of things is many. Lists are perfect tools to free us from the prison of representation precisely *because* they are so inexpressive. They decline traditional artifice, instead using mundaneness to offer "a brief intimation of everything."[21]

Perhaps the problem is not with lists but with literature, whose preference for traditional narrative acts as a correlationist amplifier. Whether empathy or defamiliarization is its goal, literature aspires for identification, to create resonance between readers and the human characters in a work. Lists work differently. Consider this one, which appears in Roland Barthes's delightfully strange auto-biography:

J'aime, je n'aime pas ~ I like, I don't like

I like: salad, cinnamon, cheese, pimento, marzipan, the smell of new-cut hay (why doesn't someone with a "nose" make such a perfume), roses, peonies, lavender, champagne, loosely held political convictions, Glenn Gould, too-cold beer, flat pillows, toast, Havana cigars, Handel, slow walks, pears, white peaches, cherries, colors, watches, all kinds of writing pens, desserts, unrefined salt, realistic novels, the piano, coffee, Pollock, Twombly, all romantic music, Sartre, Brecht, Verne, Fourier, Eisenstein, trains, Médoc wine, having change, *Bouvard and Pécuchet*, walking in sandals on the lanes of southwest France, the bend of the Adour seen from Doctor L.'s house, the Marx Brothers, the mountains at seven in the morning leaving Salamanca, etc.

I don't like: white Pomeranians, women in slacks, geraniums, strawberries, the harpsichord, Miró, tautologies, animated cartoons, Arthur Rubinstein, villas, the afternoon, Satie, Bartók, Vivaldi, telephoning, children's choruses, Chopin's concertos, Burgundian branles and Renaissance dances, the organ, Marc-Antoine Charpentier, his trumpets and kettle-drums, the politico-sexual, scenes, initiatives, fidelity, sponta-neity, evenings with people I don't know, etc.[22]

Like literary prose, the account is meant to help the reader grasp something about Barthes, yet by fashioning a list he also draws our attention to the curious world outside his person, as filtered through the arbitrary meter of likes and dislikes. Unlike his literary and criti-cal works, this list disrupts being, spilling a heap of unwelcome and incoherent crap at the foot of the reader. In doing so, a tiny part of the expanding universe is revealed through cataloging.

Ontographical cataloging hones a virtue: the abandonment of

anthropocentric narrative coherence in favor of worldly detail. Quasi-ontographical prototypes are common throughout literature and the arts, where catalogs and lists pepper a narrative, disrupting a story with unexpected piquancy. The catalog of ships in book 2 of Homer's *Iliad* offers one example, its inventory of the Achaean navy covering some 265 lines of the epic and detailing over one thousand ships from fifty different locales carrying well over a hundred different nationalities.[23] Similarly, Herman Melville's *Moby-Dick* catalogs the equipment and practices of nineteenth-century whaling as much as it does a story of obsession and revenge. A characteristic excerpt:

> The lower subdivided part, called the junk, is one immense honeycomb of oil, formed by the crossing and re-crossing, into ten thousand infiltrated cells, of tough elastic white fibres throughout its whole extent. The upper part, known as the Case, may be regarded as the great Heidelburgh Tun of the Sperm Whale. And as that famous great tierce is mystically carved in front, so the whale's vast plaited forehead forms innumerable strange devices for the emblematical adornment of his wondrous tun. Moreover, as that of Heidelburgh was always replenished with the most excellent of the wines of the Rhenish valleys, so the tun of the whale contains by far the most precious of all his oily vintages; namely, the highly-prized spermaceti, in its absolutely pure, limpid, and odoriferous state. Nor is this precious substance found unalloyed in any other part of the creature. Though in life it remains perfectly fluid, yet, upon exposure to the air, after death, it soon begins to concrete; sending forth beautiful crystalline shoots, as when the first thin delicate ice is just forming in water.[24]

Passages like this are frequent and detailed enough to match the travails of Ishmael, Queequeg, Ahab, and others on the Pequod. It would be just as appropriate to call *Moby-Dick* a natural history as it would a novel—the former is perhaps more apt, even.

A truly deliberate—not to mention lucid and beautiful—specimen of inventory ontography can be found in the Brazilian bossa nova, a form of soft jazz that evolved from samba in the mid-twentieth century. Just as Spufford's written lists make a break with literary tradition in form as much as in content, bossa nova's structure differs considerably from other musical forms. It softens the swing rhythm of jazz into a gentler sway. And unlike samba, bossa nova has no dance step; it's designed to be heard rather than felt. Furthermore, the structure of pop music finds no place in bossa nova, where repetitive, whispery, lyrical verses take the place of the narrative verse-chorus-bridge structure.

"The Girl from Ipanema" is probably the best-known example, with its tiny catalog of properties—"tall and tan and young and lovely"—but Tom Jobim's "Águas de Março" ("Waters of March") is the ultimate ontographic bossa nova collage. Each line begins with "É" ("It's" in the English version, which Jobim also wrote) and names one or two objects. A wide variety of things are mentioned in the song, from natural objects (stick, stone, oak, fish) to human-made ones (spear, truck, bricks, gun) to concepts (must, bet, loss, nothing). The song's lyrics could be interpreted as a gentle memento mori, detailing the passing of life into and out of prosperity, but the song's rhythm and tone give the lie to that sort of moralism.

Instead, the "Waters of March" name the torrential rains of Rio de Janeiro, bossa nova's birthplace. The deluge floods the streets, dredging up and making visible the myriad things seen and unseen in normal conditions. Here's a sample (note that the English version differs from the Portuguese in some verses):

É pau, é pedra,	A stick, a stone,
é o fim do caminho	It's the end of the road,
É um resto de toco,	It's the rest of a stump,
é um pouco sozinho	It's a little alone
É um caco de vidro,	It's a sliver of glass,
é a vida, é o sol	It is life, it's the sun,
É a noite, é a morte,	It is night, it is death,
é um laço, é o anzol	It's a trap, it's a gun
É peroba do campo,	The oak when it blooms,
é o nó da madeira	A fox in the brush,
Caingá, candeia,	A knot in the wood,
é o Matita Pereira	The song of a thrush

É madeira de vento,	The wood of the wind,
tombo da ribanceira	A cliff, a fall,
É o mistério profundo,	A scratch, a lump,
é o queira ou não queira	It is nothing at all

"Waters of March" does real ontological work. By setting the objects of "it" to a wide variety of different things, it gives sonorous voice to flat ontology. In a verse like the one below, we find the juxtaposition of a human-made, aggregate object, a natural condition, an action, and a concept:

> A truckload of bricks
> in the soft morning light,
> The shot of a gun
> in the dead of the night

Perhaps this incredible flexibility and openness toward things of all sorts explains why "Waters of March" has been frequently appropriated as a platform for communicating ontological repleteness. A somewhat less object-oriented version of the song made an appearance in a 1985 Coca-Cola ad, which declared, "It's a kick, it's a hit, it's a Coke, Coke is it."[25] The *it's* of "Waters of March" offers the marketer a perfect translation of the Coca-Cola Company's hopes for the famous slogan that appears in their commercial rendition of Jobim's bossa nova. No matter the situation, a cold Coca-Cola has a place.

More recently, the San Francisco–based television advertising director Carl Willat made an unauthorized, self-promotional television commercial for the American specialty grocer Trader Joe's (which famously refuses to air advertisements).[26] Unlike Coke's thirty-second spot, Willat's homage runs for nearly three minutes, recreating the entirety of "Waters of March" in reference to the curious and wonderful things that occupy Trader Joe's. A selection of verses from Willat's short film:

> It's milk, it's bread
> It's the stuff on your list
> It's the strange little snacks

you end up buying instead
It's a box of soup
It's a bell from a boat
It's yogurt made
from the milk of a goat
A handle that rips
on a paper sack
That checker you like
who'll never be back
It's the plastic grapes
hanging over the wine
It's the guy with twelve items
in the ten item line
It's the beautiful moms
in their yoga clothes
It's your favorite place
it's that store Trader Joe's

Willat's adaptation characterizes the store effectively because he recognizes that a great wealth of objects constitute it—not just the products but also the queues, the parking lot, the product discontinuations, the customers, the decor. This may seem like a prosaic observation to make in print, but watching the video produces a sensation of surprise: the experience of Trader Joe's is not just that of the shopper but also that of the shelving, the managerial policy, the secretive economics, the aloe chunk juice. Lists of objects without explication can do the philosophical work of drawing our attention toward them with greater attentiveness.

VISUAL ONTOGRAPHS

Verbal lists like Latour litanies and "Waters of March" teach us that the specificity of objects well up when situations are concretized and enumerated. Yet these examples are fleeting, the exceptions that prove the rule. How might such a strategy be carried out on a larger scale?

One such effort can be found in François Blanciak's speculative, paradigmatic architectural theory *Siteless*. In a series of 1,001 rectilinear sketches, all drawn freehand "for the sake of versatility," Blanciak offers a hypothetical account of abstracted interedifice relations as they might exist in some hypothetical alien cityscape. The forms are all identical in size, with no sense of scale to distinguish office tower from iron sculpture from garden slug. Within each, he suggests (but does not clarify) formal, material, aesthetic, and representational implications of hypothetical structures. For example, the "optician building" illustrates a reading chart inscribed into the face of a tall rectangular structure; the "pixel circle" depicts a blocky "O" shape that appears much thinner than it is wide; the "inflatable floors" sketch shows a log cabin–like shape composed of puffy layers; and the "house arena" details an open space produced by unfolding the sides of a canonical house form into hinged surfaces (see Figure 2).[27]

While architecture has embraced the optical illusion of material deformation since the rise of architectural deconstructivism, that style's characteristic shapes often fail to contrast the form of a structure with the malleability of a material. Frank Gehry's Walt Disney Concert Hall and Dancing House insinuate motion and gesture, but it is difficult to experience such works as spatial organisms both supple and rigid all at once. After the construction of the Disney Concert Hall, nearby residents complained about the hot, blinding reflections that issued from the building's polished stainless steel surface. Perhaps this result came about not because Gehry had failed to take the surrounding neighborhood into account (as he is often criticized for doing) but because he had failed to consider the building as an ontograph of sun, cushion, and steel.

optician building

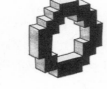

pixel circle

inflatable floors

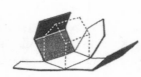

house arena

FIGURE 2. Four of the more than one thousand abstract architectural forms in François Blanciak's architectural treatise *Siteless*, which offers "an open-ended compendium of visual ideas for the architectural imagination to draw from."

By contrast, Blanciak's sketches offer a simultaneity of material and form that brings together unfamiliar objects implausibly, often in materially impossible relation. The "floor bud," for example, offers a series of surfaces gathered together in the form of a rose. The simultaneity of forms suggests different object relations, within and without the domain of architectural reality: petal as substrate for insect, for raindrop; floor as housing for wood, for metal, for rat, for copper wire. All together, the 1,001 takes on simultaneous abstract objects provide ontographies of unrelated objects, akin to Latour litanies but with implied if speculative material couplings between unfamiliar entities.

As Lynch describes it, "Ontography would involve . . . mundane, deflationary transformation."[28] Such mutations already appear in Latour's litanies and in Blanciak's speculative hybrid forms, but something overly remarkable is still going on in both cases. Mullahs and monsters, cushioned skyscrapers bent back on themselves—these are all fantastical inscriptions. Moreover, they are scarce and precious: the occasional devotional interlude in a study of bacteria, a scant example of a fleeting experimental structural design.

For a more ordinary alternative, consider the photography of Stephen Shore. He is an artist best known for two things, documenting Andy Warhol's Factory in the mid-1960s and popularizing color photography as a fine arts practice in the 1970s. But such a characterization ignores the remarkable creativity in Shore's photographs.

Fifty years before Shore, Brassaï had dragged a foldable plate camera with tripod and magnesium powder lights around Paris—a process anyone who has climbed the steps of Montmartre might find more remarkable than his famous image of them. Yet at a time when Henri Cartier-Bresson and Garry Winogrand's tiny Leica rangefinders still set the standard for the subtle documentation of the outside world, Shore returned to the film plates of Brassaï's era. It might be tempting to imagine a photographic version of Latour litanies that involve innumerable images, the sort of strategy Winogrand brought to street photography. But Shore did the opposite, making precious few photographs with an 8 × 10 view camera he lugged across North America.[29]

Today, photography has become so commonplace that we scarcely think about its equipment, except perhaps to compare statistics on the latest gadget. But Shore's photography cannot be fully appreciated without an understanding of the nature of the view camera. To take a photograph with one, the photographer must set up the device and frame its image on a ground glass plate inserted in the film back. The lens projects onto the film plane upside down, requiring the photographer to compose and focus in a way that is decidedly unlike the way we normally think of photography, as an unmediated way of looking. Once composed, the photographer replaces the ground glass with emulsion and uses a wired release to trip the shutter and expose the film. The process invites the artist to see the scene to be captured separately from the way the camera will see it. It offers a phenomenal parallax that already invites curiosity toward the objects in the scene: the view through the ground glass is not only rotated but also translated from the photographer's natural vantage point.

Brassaï composed and recomposed, watching the image on ground glass before capturing and later obsessing over the edges of his frames for perfection. The same is true of Ansel Adams, who also used view cameras to capture America's dynamical sublime. Both sought to overcome the perceptual parallax of the view camera by producing the most humanlike perspective possible, usually an idealized view. Everything finds its place: black lampposts in relief against the mist wafting up the *escalier de Montmartre*, the Snake River winding carefully back and forth toward the snowcapped Tetons, a young girl carefully hidden in the shadows of a corner shop's eaves. All inspire, invoke, or reinforce our ordinary, human experience of these objects and scenes.

But Shore composes entirely different images. It is easy to say that the subjects—city streets and motels mostly—are *more* mundane, but to be fair, the streets of Paris before the war and Wyoming before the Jackson Hole National Monument were also mundane in their eras. Shore's images are deflationary not because their subjects are subordinate but because their composition underscores unseen things and relations (Plates 1a–c).

In New York City, a television sits atop a pale orange table. Nearby rest glass bottles and some sort of frame wrapped in paper. The television's single antenna extends to the side, crossing in front of the tallest bottle.

In Rolla, Missouri, a water fountain perches in a semi-
circular alcove, its drain pipe extending to the right and into
the wall behind, while its power cord attaches to an outlet just
above its basin.

In Alberta, a textured, rust-colored lamp with shade
sits near the edge of a table, while an ashtray holds down a
motel survey. Nearby, a window lever emerges from behind
curtains.[30]

These images register the world.[31] As Michael Fried explains, the
images are remarkable because Shore's relation to the subject is
unironic. "You don't seem superior to the material. Nor are you seeing these places and things as a foreigner might," suggests Fried to
Shore in an interview.[32] The result, Fried suggests, is "imaginatively
liberating." They posit objects, even the objects of human activity, in
a world of mysterious relation with one another.

Consider one of his most famous images. At the corner of Beverly and La Brea in Los Angeles, a Chevron station sits across from
a Texaco (Plate 2). While the composition suggests the familiar vantage point of a pedestrian, the view itself bears little resemblance
to the street photographer's usual focus on human activity. An im-
mense swath of pavement occupies most of the bottom of the image,
drawing attention to the pneumatic cable that stretches in front of
the pumps. It curls like a pig's tail. In the center of the frame, plastic numerals attach to a sign to indicate prices. Below them, a soft
vinyl tube contains radial tires, the form of which gives the tube its
shape. Just behind, a station wagon's transmission assembly extends
down from its chassis, almost reaching the painted asphalt surface
of a crosswalk. Everywhere, all across the image, objects tousle one
another.

To list them underscores the difference between a Latour litany
and a Shore ontograph: floodlight, screen print, Mastercard, rubber,
asphalt, taco, Karmann Ghia, waste bin, oil stain. The Latour litany
gathers disparate things together like a strong gravitational field. But
the Shore ontograph takes things already gathered and explodes
them into their tiny, separate, but contiguous universes. As Christy
Lange explains, "This was a new conception of the landscape picture, one in which the details themselves—their density and abun-

dance, rather than their entirety—were intended to be the focal point or subject."[33] Nothing is overlooked, nothing reduced to anything else, nothing given priority. Instead, everything sits suspended.

Other photographs invite greater specificity. On an outdoor dining table at a McDonald's in Perrine, Florida, a partly eaten hamburger rests inside a polystyrene box (Plate 3). Fries and a cup of ice milk sit atop a napkin, while deep scratches on the table below reveal a pink surface beneath yellow paint. In this image, Shore focuses our attention not on the gastronomical relation between lunch and hunger, or on the industrial relation between franchise and customer, or even on the amorous relation between a previous diner and an unseen girl called Jenny, whose name has been scratched into the table's cold surface. Instead, units reveal themselves: pickle dangles across meat patty, salt scuttles from fry, ice milk clings to the inside of plastic straw. It is a common image for Shore, the secret lives of meals.

But ontographically speaking, this image tells us nothing about the perception of milk on plastic, seed on bun. It simply catalogs, like the monk's bestiary, exemplifying the ways that human intervention can never entirely contain the mysterious alien worlds of objects. Like painting, photography usually operates on the temporal scale of *now*. The landscape or the still life shows the corporeal arrangements of things, arrested before human perception. But Shore's work rejects the singularity of the now in favor of the infinity of the *meanwhile*.

EXPLODED VIEWS

Meanwhile is a powerful ontographical tool. The unit is both a system and a set. Under normal conditions, its state remains jumbled, inconspicuous, unseen in its withdrawal. In its most raw form, the Latour litany offers an account of a segment of being. It's an *account* in the literal sense of the word, like a ledger keeps the financial books. The practice of ontography—and it is a practice, not merely a theory— describes the many processes of *accounting for* the various units that strew themselves throughout the universe. To create an ontograph involves cataloging things, but also drawing attention to the couplings of and chasms between them. The tire and chassis, the ice milk and cup, the buckshot and soil: things like these exist not just *for us* but

also *for themselves* and *for one another*, in ways that might surprise
and dismay us. Such is the ontographical project, to draw attention
to the countless things that litter our world unseen. As Harman puts
it in his application of the term, *ontography* is "a name . . . for the
exercise of describing and classifying pairings" of objects.[34] Harman's
use is different from mine (he uses "ontography" to describe the relations between what he calls real and sensual qualities of objects), but
the spirit is the same: "Rather than a geography dealing with stock
natural characters such as forests and lakes, ontography maps the
basic landmarks and fault lines in the universe of objects."[35]

We can analogize the spirit of ontography with a technique in
graphic and information design, the *exploded view* diagram. Such
drawings are commonly found today in parts manuals, assembly
instructions, technical books, posters, and other diagrams meant to
"show the mating relationships of parts, subassemblies, and higher
assemblies."[36] But the technique dates back to the Renaissance, as
even a cursory review of Leonardo da Vinci's notebooks reveals.

The exploded-view drawing is meant to clarify some complex
physical system for the benefit of a human constructor, operator,
or designer (Figure 3). But in common practice, an exploded-view
drawing offers just as much intrigue as it does use value: for example,
when viewing a car parts manual, someone with no knowledge of

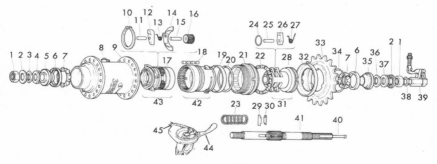

FIGURE 3. Exploded-view diagrams show both sides of being, density,
and expansion. This example shows the components of a Shimano
three-speed internal gear hub for a bicycle. Among the several dozen
parts that constitute it are a cone stay washer (4), a planet pinion (16),
and a pawl spring (27).

automotive repair can still bask in the unfamiliar repleteness present in a modern automobile. Likewise, a child pores over the cutaway view of the submarine unfolded from a magazine not to learn how to operate it but to fathom a small aspect of its murky otherworldliness.

They are not identical, but the exploded view and the ontograph have much in common. An anonymous, unseen situation of things is presented in a way that effectively draws our attention to its configurative nature. An ontograph records the presence of many potential unit operations, a profusion of particular perspectives on a particular set of things.

It's no wonder, then, that photography offers such good examples—the photograph has long been understood as a "way of looking." On the one hand, it offers a view of the world that is representational, thanks to the photographer's framing and choice of exposure. On the other hand, it offers an automatically encyclopedic rendition of a scene, thanks to the photographic apparatus's ability to record actuality. Shore's enormous plate film is particularly adept at such renditions, able to capture vast detail at high resolution. Not every photograph is an ontograph, but Shore's work tends in this direction, partly because he refuses to treat any object as primary, as a subject. "Beverly Boulevard and La Brea Avenue" regards nothing in particular and everything all at once. Shore's framing technique turns his photographs into ontographs.

ONTOGRAPHIC MACHINES

Photographic ontography is effective as art and as metaphysics. But photographs are static; they *imply* but do not *depict* unit operations. For the latter, we must look to artifacts that themselves operate.

Many puzzle toys and games are abstract: Rubik's Cube, *Tetris*, and *Bejeweled* ask players to manipulate shapes and figures to complete goals. Cube faces, polyominoes, and gem tokens are certainly real objects, but they are also units removed from context such that their associations with other units become indistinct. But other games are concrete, mapping abstract gestures to concrete meanings. The popular puzzle board game *Rush Hour* is such a one. The game is played on a gray plastic grid onto which molded automobiles of various sizes can be arranged. The player attempts to extract a red car through an opening in the side of the game board by moving the other vehicles out of its way. Cars and trucks can be moved only by sliding them backward or forward along their axis of orientation. The game comes with many dozens of puzzle cards, which describe initial states of the board for the player to solve, each becoming more difficult than the last.

Rush Hour could have been created with abstract colored blocks instead of vehicles. The experience of playing the game would remain the same, on a mechanical level at least. On a representational level, however, its meaning would become indeterminate. Just imagine an abstract Stephen Shore–style ontograph, with multicolored, three-dimensional polyhedrons taking the place of tire stack, station wagon, traffic light, and all of the many other objects in the picture. Such an artifact might be interesting as art, particularly if it re-created the overall form of a real scene, but it would likely not be ontographical in the same way as the original. The addition of a fictional skin connects the mechanical operation of the abstract game to the material reality of a specific unit operation—in this case traffic congestion. If the fictional skin and the mechanical depth are tightly coupled, then the resulting game can offer a compelling account of an ontological domain.[37]

Rush Hour offers a good example of tight coupling, but its scope is more limited than a Latour litany or a Shore ontograph: only car and road appear in the game. *Scribblenauts* offers a more encyclopedic account of things. It's an unusual videogame created by the developer 5th Cell and released for the Nintendo DS handheld in 2009. On first glance, the game looks like any other 2-D platform or adventure game. The player controls a cute, pixelated character named Maxwell. Each of its two hundred levels takes place in an abstraction of a realistic environment, be it city, ice floe, mine, or ocean. Somewhere in the level sits a "Starite" (a shiny star icon), which the player must collect to complete the level. The challenge comes in reaching the starite, a task troubled by one of two challenges, depending on the game mode. In puzzle levels, the player must help Maxwell complete a task to reveal the starite: return soil samples to the astronaut; fill and pay for a tray of cafeteria food; stop the out-of-control truck. In action levels, the player must help

Maxwell capture a starite placed out of reach: atop a tree, perhaps, or across a lake, or underground, for example.

To overcome such challenges, the player can summon objects into the level by typing their names into a notebook in the game. The game recognizes almost anything—its dictionary includes some 22,800 terms, from air raid shelter to zucchini.[38] After the player types a word that the game recognizes, the requested object drops into the game, bearing an appearance *and* behavior befitting its name. The player can then move, connect, operate, and manipulate these objects to complete the game's puzzles.

Scribblenauts puzzles ask the player to retrieve only the starite, but they also offer incentives to explore the operational possibility space formed by the level scenario along with the many thousands of summonable objects. Some of these incentives are codified in the game itself: after completing a level, the game awards "merits" for meeting certain criteria (e.g., "entomologist" for using two or more insects, or "savior" for completing a level without harming any humanoids or animals).[39] Playing a level three times without reusing objects earns a gold star.

But even absent these explicit incentives, the game still inspires natural curiosity. Despite its incredibly bare-bones simulation of individual and interobject behaviors, *Scribblenauts* still motivates players to explore a multitude of unit operations by sheer force of charm. In the game's eleventh puzzle level, the player must collect three flowers without harming them or the girl whose basket awaits them. One flower is guarded by a bee, one sits underwater near a piranha, and one sits precipitously atop a ledge. Innumerable permutations of unit operations exist for completing the puzzle, some portion of which the average player will explore in a single session. Here are the some of the sixteen attempts the critic Stephen Totilo tried before completing the level:

Attempt 3: Made bear; bear killed bee. Laid down bear trap, ran away. Bear didn't chase. Ran back over. Caught self in bear trap. Mauled by bear. Level failed.

Attempt 6: Made exterminator. Exterminator fumigated bee. Did not grab first flower. Approached piranha lake. Made fish-ing boat. Dropped big boat into lake. Boat must have crushed flower. Level failed.

Attempt 10: Made gun. Tried to shoot bee dead. Bullet ricocheted and destroyed first flower. Level failed.

Attempt 12: Made hot air balloon. Put Maxwell in it. Flew over piranha lake. Made gun. Shot at fish. Gun destroyed hot air balloon instead. Fell into lake. Jumped out of lake. Made corpse. Threw it into lake to draw fish away. Made gun to shoot fish while it ate corpse. Shots didn't hit. Made new corpse and tried with sniper rifle. Didn't work. Dove in and just grabbed flower. Success. Bee was gone. Put lake flower in basket. Put bee flower in basket. Made helicopter to get to high ridge for final flower. Was afraid to land helicopter on ledge, out of fear of destroying flower. Tried to jump out of helicopter. Fell into piranha lake. Died. Level failed.

Attempt 13: Made gun. Shot bee dead. Got first flower. Made two corpses. Tossed them into piranha lake for distraction. Dove and recovered second flower. Made truck and dumped it into lake. Did same with a boat. Tried climbing over those vehicles to get to ledge and final flower. Vehicles shifted; Maxwell thrown into ridge wall. Died. Level failed.

Attempt 16. Made gun. Shot bee dead. Made hot air balloon. Flew to ridge. Got out, grabbed flower. Got back in balloon. Safely put cliff flower in basket. Put bee flower in basket. Threw corpses into piranha lake to distract fish. Dove in and grabbed lake flower. Jumped out. Put lake flower in basket. Starite found! Success![40]

Shore's photographs catalog the way things *exist* in a given situation. *Scribblenauts* catalogs the way things *work* in one. Both approaches explode the density of being, giving viewer and player a view of a tiny sliver of the infinity of being, through reconfiguration.

WHAT'S IN A WORD?

A Latour litany reveals a few unfamiliar corners of being's infinity through naming. *Scribblenauts* reveals objects' relations by inspiring players to invoke their behaviors in relation to one another, by keying in the signs that name them. In both cases, language works referentially, identifying an object such that the edges of its experience can be imagined or explored.

But language itself is composed of things. Words do not just denote, they also operate. We can understand *signs themselves* to have experiences of one another that remain comprehensible only by tracing their own relations to our engagement with them as signifiers. Latour litanies already lead us to the river of semiotic ontology, offering brochures of semantic units—words—as much as of material ones. In that respect, grammatical incantations like the recitation of Latin declensions function ontographically, as an informal catalog of the varieties of grammatical case possible with a linguistic domain: *puella, puellae, puellae, puellam, puella.* But more complex examples of linguistic ontography require more detailed, deliberate artifacts that expose the strange graspings of stuffs linguistic.

Take *In a Pickle,* a card game about words. Play is simple: each card is emblazoned with a word, and under the word is an arrow pointing downward. The players are dealt five such cards each, and four more are placed face up on the table. On each turn, a player selects a card and places it atop one of the outermost cards in a pile. For such a play to be valid, the word on the card played must either fit *inside* or be *larger* than the outermost card onto which it is played, or be able to be fit *inside* or be *smaller* than the innermost card. For example, given the starting card "Dryer," "Basement" could be played atop it, on the outside. Then "Shirt" could be placed underneath "Dryer," on the inside. Play proceeds like this until a row contains four cards, in which case players take turns playing one last card that is larger than the outermost card in the pile (see Figure 4). The game continues until one player captures a winning number of sets (the winning total varies based on the number of players).

The game instructions encourage players to "think creatively and play cards that might not 'fit' in an obvious way." Players can challenge such "creative" interpretations, and opponents vote to allow or invalidate them. The designers offer such an example in the rules: "Yes, you can fit a Turkey in a Purse. It's sliced turkey."

In a Pickle is based on homography. In linguistics, homographs

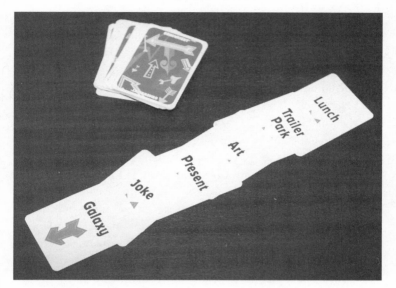

FIGURE 4. A round of *In a Pickle* in progress. Note how the chain combines physical and conceptual objects at various scales.

are two different words that share the same orthography yet have different meanings. For example, "bark" (the sound a dog makes) and "bark" (the surface of a tree) are homographs. Homographs are helpful lenses for tiny ontology, which maintains that being multiplies and expands. *Bark* the name for a dog's sound and *bark* the name for a woody surface are different units (remember, we're talking about the *signifiers* as much as the signifieds). Yet *bark* is another thing entirely, a sign that can mean several things to an English speaker, among them the sound of a dog and the covering of a tree. (For that matter, *bark* is also an instance of that sign, which appears in the present sentence.)

Moves far more interesting than "Turkey in a Purse" are possible in the game, thanks to the mereological possibility space afforded by homography. As the game's title suggests, a Fork could be in a Pickle, but a Bank Robber could as well. For that matter, a Movie could be in a Pickle (when "Movie" is as a metonym for its production), and yet a Pickle could be in a Movie (when "Pickle" is a prop). So could a Bank Robber. Indeed, a Pickle could be in a Bank Robber in a Pickle in a Movie in a Pickle.

Things just get weirder: A Movie could be in a Letter ("I just saw this strange movie about an incompetent, vinegar-loving bank robber"), which could be in an Atlas (as a bookmark), which could be in a Tornado, in a Dream, in a Woman, in a Marriage. Or better, a Movie could be in the Universe, which could nevertheless *also* be in a letter ("I wouldn't give up pickles for anything in the world"), in the Mail, in Time.

A Latour litany is an ontograph made of words. By contrast, *In a Pickle* is a machine for producing ontographs *about* words. It bears the tagline, "The what's in a word game," and in this case "in a word" means two things. For one, it takes on the idiomatic sense of "briefly" or "in a nutshell." Indeed, nutshellery isn't a bad metaphor for tiny ontology—the condensation of multitudes into dense singularities. For another, it implies containment. Words have semantic extensions for human speakers, and playing with homographs can reveal those extensions. But containment also takes yet another, even more curious meaning. "In a word" can refer to the interior of a semantic unit, the molten core of a name, where its various homographs and referents swim like ribosomes grazing on peptide chains.

A Latour litany helps catalog material, conceptual, and fictional objects; *In a Pickle* shows us how ontography can be performed on far more abstract units. If a dictionary shows us the meaning of words *for us*, the game attempts the opposite: to reveal that words have meaning *for themselves*. A dictionary is a catalog of the meanings of words. But *In a Pickle* is a catalog of the insides of words, like a crossword puzzle is a dictionary of the letters between them.

Dictionaries, grocery stores, Rio de Janeiro, La Brea, and Beverly— these are the labels we stick to the outsides of things. They mark them with relevance, but they also occlude the richness of their infinite depths. Ontography is a practice of increasing the number and density, one that sometimes opposes the minimalism of contemporary art. Instead of removing elements to achieve the elegance of simplicity, ontography adds (or simply leaves) elements to accomplish the realism of multitude. It is a practice of exploding the innards of things—be they words, intersections, shopping malls, or creatures. This "explosion" can be as figurative or as literal as you like, but it must above all reveal the hidden density of a unit.

For the ontographer, Aristotle was wrong: nature does not operate in the shortest way possible but in a multitude of locally streamlined yet globally inefficient ways.[41] Indeed, an obsession with simple explanations ought to bother the metaphysician. Instead of worshipping simplicity, OOO embraces messiness. We must not confuse the values of the *design* of objects for human use, such as doors, toasters, and computers, with the *nature* of the world itself. An ontograph is a crowd, not a cellular automaton that might describe its emergent operation. An ontograph is a landfill, not a Japanese garden. It shows how *much* rather than how *little* exists simultaneously, suspended in the dense meanwhile of being:

On August 10, 1973, at a boathouse in Southwest Houston, the shovel of a police forensics investigator struck the femur of one of seventeen corpses excavated that week, victims of serial killer Dean Corll.

Meanwhile, 235 nautical miles above the earth's surface, a radio wave began its course from Skylab to a parabolic radar dish antenna aboard United States Naval Ship Vanguard.

Meanwhile, at Royals Stadium in Kansas City, Lou Piniella's cleat met home plate, kicking up dust as it scored what would become the team's winning run against the Baltimore Orioles.

And meanwhile, at the Trail's End Restaurant in Kanab, Utah, a bowl snuggled a half cantaloupe, and butter seeped into the caramelized surface of a pancake (Plate 4).

[3]

METAPHORISM

Speculating about the
Unknowable Inner Lives of Units

Meanwhile in mind, consider for a moment some of the things that are happening somewhere, right now:

Smoke vacuums through the valve, grommet, and hose of a hookah and enters a pursed mouth.

The dog teeth of a collar engage a gear against the layshaft coupling of a transmission assembly.

The soluble cartilage of a chicken neck decocts from the bone into the stock of a consommé.

These and other interactions between objects constitute different moves in the material world. From our human perspective, they correspond with actions we know well: smoking, shifting, or cooking. Traditionally, a human's first-person experience of such interactions would offer clear subjects for phenomenological inquiry; not only perception and thought but also memory and emotion: the taste of the honey-sweet ma'sal heated under the charcoal in the hookah's bowl, or the sensation of foot on clutch as the collar of the synchro obtains a friction catch on the gear, or the smooth, thin appearance of broth as it separates from fat and bone in the soup pot. But for the hookah, the gear, or the chicken, what's going on? Or likewise for Shore's cantaloupe or ice milk or water glass? And how might we understand those relations?

A tempting answer might be *science*. We could evaluate the surface tension of the melon rind, determine the indentation hardness of porcelain, measure the condensation point of vapor against ice-water glass, or describe the rotational force of gear in relation to transmission lever. But unlike the jobs of horticulturists, physicists, or forest rangers, alien phenomenology is not a practice of scientific naturalism, seeking to define the physical or causal relations between objects. To do so would take things for constituents. As Bruno Latour puts it, science "is forced to explain one marvel with another, and that one with a third. It goes on until it looks just like a fairy tale."[1]

In his famous 1974 essay, the philosopher of mind Thomas Nagel attempts to answer the question "What is it like to be a bat?"[2] In Nagel's account, consciousness has a subjective character that cannot be reduced to its physical components. Physical reductionist positions hope to erase the subjectivity of experience by explaining it away via underlying physical evidences. For example, a reductionist explanation of the sweet taste of a Hostess Twinkie might involve a chemosensory account of how the compounds that make up the treat bind with a biomolecular substrate on the taste buds, which a human eater interprets via a set of neurological receptors.[3] Nagel points out a problem with reductionist explanations like this one: even if the experience of the Twinkie can be understood as a neurochemical unit operation, such an explanation does not describe the *experience* of sweetness.

When separated from the various forms that might produce it, Nagel calls this encounter "the subjective character of experience."[4] That character, he suggests, entails "what it is like to *be* that organism." For Nagel, the very idea of experience requires this "being-likeness," a feature that eludes observation even if its edges can be traced by examining physical properties. Because of this elusiveness (which OOO calls *withdrawal*), physical reductionism can never explain the experience of a being.

The bat serves as an effective example, because we know that bats experience the world thoroughly unlike humans (despite being mammals) or birds (despite being flying creatures). Bats use echolocation to form an understanding of spaces around them, their own modulated cries acting as a kind of sonar. Even though we sometimes call them "blind," bats have a very lucid and detailed sense of space—it's just a sense that's totally alien from a human perspective.

As Nagel puts it, "Bat sonar, though clearly a form of percep
not similar in its operation to any sense that we possess, and there
is no reason to suppose that it is subjectively like anything we can
experience or imagine."[5] The best we can do is to try to conjure what
it might be like to be a bat, and in that task we will always fail, given
that imagining what it's like to be a bat is not the same as *being* a bat.

Even though Nagel's article is really about the mind–body problem, it offers a great deal of instruction in alien phenomenology. On
the one hand, phenomena are objective, often easily measured, re-
corded, or otherwise identified by some external observer. On the
other hand, such an observer cannot have the experience that corresponds with those phenomena, no matter how much evidence he or
she might collect from its event horizon.[6] As tiny ontology demands,
the character of the experience of something is not identical to the
characterization of that experience by something else. Or as Nagel
puts it, "I want to know what it is like for a *bat* to be a bat. Yet if I try
to imagine this, I am restricted to the resources of my own mind,
and those resources are inadequate to the task." Counterintuitive
though it may seem, the characterization of an experience through
supposedly objective evidence and external mechanisms leads us
farther from, not closer to, an understanding of the experience of
an entity.

The result is simple but profound: even if evidence from outside a thing (be it bat, hookah, or cantaloupe) offers clues to how
it perceives, the experience of that perception remains withdrawn.
This state of affairs poses a problem for modern science. Scientific
discoveries have a magical flavor, offering lurid descriptions of how
things "really" work.[8] And those magical discoveries may even describe some of the effects of object interactions. But to understand
how something operates on its surroundings, or they on it, is not the
same as understanding how that other thing *understands* those operations. The unit operation that comprises the bat's sonar perception
exists separately from the bat's grasping of that apparatus, and of the
human's grasping of that apparatus, and of the cave wall's grasping of
that apparatus, and so forth. To comprehend the effects of the high-
frequency vibrations voiced and heard by bats simply has nothing to
do with understanding what it's like to be a bat.

THE CLARITY OF DISTORTION

Nagel's goal is an "objective phenomenology," one "not dependent on empathy or the imagination."[9]

> Though presumably it would not capture everything, [objective phenomenology's] goal would be to describe, at least in part, the subjective character of experiences in a form comprehensible to beings incapable of having those experiences.
>
> We would have to develop such a phenomenology to describe the sonar experiences of bats; but it would also be possible to begin with humans. One might try, for example, to develop concepts that could be used to explain to a person blind from birth what it was like to see. . . . The loose intermodal analogies—for example, "Red is like the sound of a trumpet"—which crop up in discussion of this subject are of little use. That should be clear to anyone who has both heard a trumpet and seen red. But structural features of perception might be more accessible to objective description, even though something would be left out.[10]

Here Nagel and I disagree. The perceptions of the sighted and the blind man differ *precisely because* the former has heard a trumpet and seen red, and the latter has only heard a trumpet. The trumpet-to-redness analogy sounds unviable because it's *bad*, not because it's philosophically troublesome. Unlike objective phenomenology, alien phenomenology accepts that the subjective character of experiences cannot be fully recuperated objectively, even if it remains wholly real. In a literal sense, *the only way to perform alien phenomenology is by analogy*: the bat, for example, operates like a submarine. The redness hues like fire.

The subjectivity of these accounts might raise concern: to talk about a bat in terms of a seafaring vessel, a color in terms of a tactile sensation—moves like these feel dangerously selfish. The risk of falling into anthropocentrism is strong. Indeed, I'll take things farther: anthropocentrism is unavoidable, at least for us humans. The same is true of any unit (for the bats, chiropteracentrism is the problem). The subjective nature of experience makes the unit operation of one of its perceptions amount always to a caricature in which the one is drawn in the distorted impression of the other. This is true not only of the encounter itself but also of any account of the encounter, which only further distances the one from the other by virtue of the introduction of additional layers of mediation.

There is a considerable difference between accepting the truth of human accounts of object perceptions and recognizing that, as humans, we are destined to offer anthropomorphic metaphors for the unit operations of object perception, particularly when our intention frequently involves communicating those accounts to other humans. As Jane Bennett notes, anthropomorphizing helps us underscore the differences between ourselves and the objects around us—it helps remind us that object encounters are caricatures:

> Maybe it's worth running the risks associated with anthro-pomorphizing (superstition, the divinization of nature, romanticism) because it, oddly enough, works against anthro-pocentrism: a chord is struck between person and thing, and I am no longer above or outside a nonhuman "environment."[11]

This is not just true for bats, which Nagel rightly calls "fundamen-tally alien."[12] Bats are both ordinary and weird, but so is everything else: toilet seats, absinthe louches, seagulls, trampolines. By reveal-ing objects in relation apart from us, we rediscover and refine the method of M. R. James's haunted Professor Parkins: to release objects like ghosts from the prison of human experience. Ontography might offer a low groan to startle us from the sleep of correlationism, but it doesn't take things far enough. Once we become "mesmerized by the objects in the world," how might we proceed to understand some-thing about interobject perception?[13]

Graham Harman borrows a page from Alphonso Lingis, who takes Maurice Merleau-Ponty's idea that "things see us" even far-ther. Harman contends that things enter into negotiations with other things as much as we do with them. But there's a problem: if ob-jects recede from one another, forever enclosed in the vacuum of their individual existences, how do they ever interact? Smoke and mouth, collar and gear, cartilage and water, bat and branch, roaster and green chile, button and input bus: all seem to do things to one another. Moreover, all of these factors come together as one thing, rather than remaining forever segregated as so many dissipations, couplings, pings, bits, and charges.

In Harman's view, there is something that does not recede in objects, qualities that "sever" and allow us to "bathe in them at every moment."[14] Objects float in a sensual ether. When they interact through vicarious causation, they do so only by the means they know internally but in relation to the qualities in which they "bathe." In a move he is completely serious about, Harman equates such interaction with metaphor.[15] It's a move that solves Nagel's puzzle: we never understand the alien experience, we only ever reach for it metaphorically.

Objects try to make sense of each other through the qualities and logics they possess. When one object caricatures another, the first grasps the second in abstract, enough for the one to make some sense of the other given its own internal properties. A caricature is a rendering that captures some aspects of something else at the cost of other aspects.[16] The mechanism that facilitates this sort of alien phenomenology is not Nagel's objective instrument—one that clarifies foreign perception by removing distortion—but instead a mechanism that *welcomes* such distortion.

In 1983, for the first time since the banishment of all styles save socialist realism, new approaches to literature were presented in the USSR. The reading of "Theses on Metarealism and Conceptualism" took place at the Moscow Central House for Arts Workers, presenting several new methods that had been agitating under the surface of the Soviet literary community since the mid-1970s.[17] Among them was an extension of the approaches of Andrei Voznesensky. In contrast to such socialist realist poets as Alexander Tvardovsky, Voznesensky represented a style called *metaphorism* characterized by the exuberant metaphor ("they sell the blood of God here on tap," he wrote in homage to Michelangelo).[18] The new theses extended metaphorism from the playfulness of metaphor into "metarealism," which Mikhail Epstein describes as an "earnest attempt to capture . . . the realism of metaphor."[19] Such work strives to apprehend reality *in metaphorphosis*, rather than merely use metaphor representationally. Some lines from Ivan Zhdanov's "Region of Unexchangeable Possession" offer an example:

> Either the letters cannot be understood, or
> their grand scale is unbearable to the eye—
> what remains is the red wind in the field,
> with the name of rose on its lips.[20]

If we take seriously Harman's suggestion that relation takes place not just *like* metaphor but *as* metaphor, then an opportunity suggests itself: what if we deployed *metaphor itself* as a way to grasp alien objects' perceptions of one another. The result would bear some similarity to the Russian postmodernist adoption of metaphorism and metarealism, although I suggest those precedents as inspirations rather than models. Metaphorism offers a method for alien phenomenology that grasps at the ways objects bask metaphorically in each others' "notes" (Harman's name, following Xavier Zubíri, for the attributes of a real object) by *means of metaphor itself*, rather than by describing the effects of such interactions on the objects.[21] It offers a critical process for characterizing object perceptions.

Epstein suggests that Zhdanov's poetry "consistently disembodies the substance of objects," manifesting "pure prototypes of things."[22] Likewise, to begin a process of phenomenal metaphorism, we often must break with some of our own modes of knowing. This is a mind-bender: the Husserlian epoché brackets *human* empirical intuition, but in metaphorism we recognize that our relationship to objects is not first person; we are always once removed. It is not the *objects'* perceptions that we characterize metaphorically but the *perception itself*, which recedes just as any other object does. In doing so, we release the relation from a reduction between other objects, flattening it down onto the same ontological plane as human, gearshift, perception, or red-rosed wind. As Edmund Husserl says, "A painting is only a likeness for a likeness-constituting consciousness."[23]

HOW THE SENSOR SEES

Let's consider photography once more as an example. From early forms of writing like parchment and clay, and from fine arts like painting, we inherit misconceptions about the inscription of surfaces. The page or the canvas extends in space, allowing the scribe or painter to attack any point of the surface directly and immediately, in the way that we seem to perceive such surfaces.

Despite great differences in the tools it deploys for inscription, photography maintains the illusion of painting's surface, but it shares little with that form at a material level. A film emulsion contains silver-halide crystal grains. When struck with light, the crystal molecules release an extra electron from the bromide ion, which the positively charged silver ion attracts. The silver ion is in turn transformed into metallic silver, creating a small covering of silver on the film. When a photographic emulsion is exposed, the photons focused by an optical device hit its surface all at once, and silver regions are created all over the emulsion at different intensities, producing a faint image. A digital charge-coupled device (CCD) works in much the same way as a film emulsion, although in the place of silver crystals a CCD is covered with many light-sensitive cells that record the individual pixels of an image.

Normally, we don't concern ourselves with the process of photographic exposure, except as might be necessary to fashion a picture or to assess how one was created. The way a film emulsion or a CCD perceives an object is not merely an accident of the photographer's agency. It is a material process that deserves attention for its own sake before questions of agency, reference, meaning, or criticism enter into the picture. Like Nagel's bat, the experience of the camera cannot be reduced to the operation of its constituent parts. To understand a particular apparatus's experience, we can construct a metaphorism for it, based on evidence yielded from an analysis of its notes. Let's explore one such example.

One benefit of Henri Cartier-Bresson's rangefinder over Brassaï's plate camera is portability. Oskar Barnack's 1913 design for the 35 mm camera allowed it to adopt the small size of cinema's film rather than the large format plates of still photography, like the ones Adams and Shore used. Barnack persuaded Ernst Leitz to make a commercial prototype of the camera, which was introduced in 1925 as the Leica 1. The camera became the standard device for photography until the single-lens reflex gained popularity in the 1960s and 1970s, inheriting the handheld photographic design that remains with us today.

Yet "small" is relative. There are lots of compact digital cameras on the market, but most of them produce images of less-than-desirable quality or make advanced photographic control difficult (or both). Manufacturers have kept larger sensors in larger cameras, partly for reasons of feasibility and partly to concentrate higher-end features in their SLR models. Because of their small sensor size, these cameras often have trouble recording fine detail, especially in low light. As a result, they frequently produce noisy images with color speckling instead of smooth tones.

In recent years, manufacturers have attempted to combat this challenge by building larger sensors into smaller camera bodies. Sigma offers such a device, a compact camera that uses a larger sensor, one roughly the same size as those used in many digital SLRs (DSLRs). Sigma has produced several versions of this design, including the DP1, DP2, and DP2s, billing each as "a full spec compact camera with all the power of a DSLR."

As it turns out, the sensor in the DP cameras is not just larger than the average compact camera; it is also of a different type than the kind normally found in digital cameras of any size. Most digital cameras use an imaging technology known as a Bayer sensor. Bayer sensors have a grid of photocells that see only shades of gray. An array sits in front of the sensors with a grid of red, green, and blue filters, one for each photocell. To turn input into a normal color photograph, the device runs an algorithm that interpolates a pixel's color based on the signal in a corresponding cell and in its neighboring cells.

When using the DP series, photographers notice high detail and lack of color or luminance noise at higher light sensitivity (ISO) ratings, unlike with a Bayer sensor. Yet the colors in images seem to change as ISO increases (see Plate 5 for an example). After ruling out incorrect white balance and exposure settings, the result reveals itself to be a function of light sensitivity, not of exposure. In particular, images captured at higher film speed equivalents appear less saturated in the green hues than the same image captured at lower sensitivities.[24]

Based on this evidence, the human photographer might conclude that the device is flawed or perhaps simply a victim of an unfortunate engineering trade-off. But such a conclusion would mischaracterize the way the Sigma DP *itself* perceives the world, the subject of interest for the alien phenomenologist. Rather than ask how the equipment fails to see as its operator does, let's instead ask what characterizes its experience. To do so, we can first trace the edges of the device's qualities, nipping at the event horizon that conceals its notes from public view.

In a Bayer sensor, each photocell is sensitive to only one wavelength of light—red, green, or blue. The camera's software interpolates color based on the luminance values of a photocell and its neighbors. Sigma's camera uses a different sensor design, called the Foveon. The Foveon sensor measures all wavelengths of light at each photocell. A photosensitive material is embedded onto the silicon of the chip itself, making it possible for the sensor to record all wavelengths at once. Thus no interpolation is required. In theory, then, Foveon sensors offer both better color rendition and sharper images than Bayer sensors. (A comparison of the two sensors' different methods of operation appears in Plate 6.)

The color shifts noticeable in the resulting images arise as a consequence of the way the Foveon experiences light sensitivity. In a Bayer sensor, the increased sensitivity of an ISO increase is implemented by amplifying the sensor's signal before processing. Amplification increases both signal and noise, making both the measured luminance of each pixel and its interpolated color subject to increased error. This is why images created on Bayer sensor digital cameras exhibit increased noise at higher ISO ratings. In a Foveon sensor, the silicon *itself* is photosensitive to different wavelengths of light at different layers of the sensor. When the sensor signal is amplified for greater light sensitivity, it still uses the same method for detecting luminance. Color, however, is measured only when the light passes through the silicon to stimulate the photosensitive array below.

We might say that color shift is the Foveon's high ISO equivalent of Bayer's image noise. But the resulting sensation is unfamiliar: color shift as a consequence of higher light sensitivity feels alien to the human photographer. Why? Because the Bayer sensor's method of amplifying light sensitivity is *analogous* to that of the film emulsion, while the Foveon sensor's method of amplifying light sensitivity is not. Higher-speed films are more light sensitive because the grains of silver halide on the emulsion are larger than in slower-speed film. When photons strike the crystals, they cause a chemical reaction that creates a small covering of silver on the film. The size and distribution of these coverings vary in proportion to the size of the grain.

There is thus an analogous relationship between film grain and image noise, especially luminance noise. The stippling of Bayer image noise is aesthetically and materially coupled to the stippling of film grain, and both are produced when higher light sensitivity is introduced into the photographic process. There are no simple, photographically analogous relationships between light sensitivity and selective color shifts of the kind the Foveon exhibits.

These observations help the human photographer or optical engineer understand and respond to the camera's operation. They offer evidence for how it behaves, but they do not yet metaphorize that behavior as an alien account of the camera's own perception. Charles Maurer, a perceptual psychologist at McMaster University, offers a helpful optical parallel to explain what happens in the Foveon sensor, one that offers a concrete example of metaphorism in practice.

The human eye uses different photoreceptor cells for different light levels. In low light, the eye uses rod cells, which are sensitive to green-blue wavelengths but less sensitive to red wavelengths. In well-lit conditions, the eye uses cone cells, three types of which provide high sensitivity to red, green, and blue light. Maurer describes the Foveon's perception as analogous to *mesopic vision,* the effect that human eyes experience in dim light when our eyes are confused about which types of cells to use, resulting in a rapid switching between cones and rods. Mesopic vision is the phenomenon that makes it difficult to drive at dusk. Here's Maurer:

> In sunlight we see in colour; in moonlight we see in monochrome; in transitional "mesopic" levels of dim light we see partially in monochrome and partially in colour. When painters want to represent dim light, they portray it mesopically. . . . Film does not portray dim light in this way, nor do most digital sensors, but the Foveon sensor does. Film and digital sensors generate low levels of granular noise. When a normal amount of light strikes the film or sensor, the nois

usually hidden within the image, but when little light strikes it, the noise becomes more evident. . . . However the Foveon image sensor works differently so its granularity looks different. The Foveon shows fewer specks but replaces them with intrusions of incorrect colour. At first this reduces saturation then, at the lowest levels of sensitivity, it causes random streaks and blotches.[25]

The celebrated street photographer Garry Winogrand called a photograph "the illusion of a literal description of what the camera saw,"[26] but just as different mammals see things differently, so too do different cameras. The combination of sensor, optics, and other factors makes a particular camera "see" in a particular way. Maurer's metaphor reminds us that the camera doesn't see like a human eye. Just as the bat's experience of perception differs from our understanding of the bat's experience of perception, so the camera's experience of seeing differs from our understanding of its experience. But unlike the bat, the Foveon-equipped Sigma DP provides us with exhaust from which we can derive a phenomenal metaphor to chronicle that experience.

As with any good metaphor, it feels alien: the photographer must wrap his brain around the idea that the dimness of the Sigma DP is relative to the sensor, not the human eye. Irrespective of the underlying electro-optical mechanisms that make it behave, the sensor's perception as a whole is metaphorized as mesopicism. As light sensitivity is adjusted up on the sensor, it is as if the sensor had been shrouded in increasing levels of dusk. Such is what it's *like* to be a Foveon digital image sensor, even if this isn't what it *is* to be one.

METAPHOR AND OBLIGATION

Once object relations become metaphorized, we must take care to avoid taking the constructed metaphor for the reality of the unit operation it traces. A metaphor is just a trope, not a copy. Consider how quickly a metaphorism can be taken for what it caricatures, particularly when matters of human controversy are at work.

Large, white letters on black, a bumper sticker reads, "Soy Is Murder." It's a riff off the "Meat Is Murder" adage popular among some

animal rights proponents, a slogan itself borrowed from the pro-
vegetarian title track of the second album by the Smiths. It's tempting to read the bumper sticker as a send-up, a caustic imputation
of moral vegetarianism through backhanded reductio ad absurdum.
But further reflection might dampen an initial scoff. Is wrestling a tu-
ber from the ground or ripping a pea from its pod a sort of violence?

The criticism of selective effrontery has long plagued veganism,
whose proponents have developed several responses to the accusa-
tion. One downplays the suffering of plants by arguing that they
have no central nervous system and thus cannot experience pain like
animals can. Another points out that some plants must be eaten to
spread their seed and reproduce—fruits, for example. There's even a
name for the practice of eating only fallen seeds, frutarianism. Such
a diet is sometimes correlated with *ahimsa*, a tenet to "do no harm"
central to Buddhism, Hinduism, and particularly Jainism.

To the first response, opponents respond that such an argument
assumes that feeling-by-nervous-system is the only kind of sensation.
Others clearly exist, even if they remain unfamiliar. Plants sense the
world, too, whether to seek out light or water, or to react chemically
to external threats. To the second response, they make enjoinders to
logic: even the strictest Jainist *ahimsa* risks its own violation, since
to eat the seed is also to disrupt its final cause, the new tree. Does the
wanton destruction of a new plant qualify as harm?

No matter how we may feel about eating or abstaining from meat,
appeals to feeling and suffering exemplify the correlationist conceit:
the assumption that the rights any thing should have are the same
ones we believe we should have; that living things more like us are
more important than those less like us; and that life itself is an existence of greater worth than inanimacy. These are understandable
biases for us humans. We are mortal and fragile in specific ways, and
we worry about them.

Things become more difficult when we move beyond the animate and into the great outdoors. Metaphorism issues a strange challenge to problems of ethics. When we theorize ethical codes, they
are always ethics *for us*. Whether deontological or consequentialist,
moral standards sit on the inside of the unit *human being*; they're
part of our inner formula, situated in our molten cores. Even in the

most liberal interpretations of external responsibility, such as Emmanuel Levinas's notion of the wholly unknowable other that cannot be converted into selfhood, the object of ethics relates back to the self that maintains such responsibility. While such a principle might modulate our attitudes and intentions toward objects—be they migrant workers, cocker spaniels, or plastic sporks—it can never help explain the ethics of such objects themselves.

Metaphorism is necessarily anthropomorphic, and thus it challenges the metaphysician both to embrace and to yield the limits of humanity. When perception is at issue ("How does the digital sensor perceive the puppy?"), this is a relatively uncontroversial affair. But when it comes to action, particularly action in which the human actor is implicated, the ethics of objects quickly becomes unthinkable. Thanks to feminist studies, postcolonial studies, animal studies, environmental studies, and other accounts of human relationships with nonhuman entities, we tend to doubt that some things ought to thrive at others' expense. Today, most would accept that British men are no more intrinsically worthy of preservation and prosperity than women, Congalese, horses, and redwoods. But few would accept that fried chicken buckets, Pontiac Firebirds, and plastic picnicware deserve similar consideration (unless their existence or use might disturb people, animals, or nature). When we form these theories, we mount accounts of why and how humans ought to behave in and toward the universe, but not about how other objects ought to behave in relation to it.

It's possible to generalize, of course. For example, one could argue that no matter what sort of thing a unit is, it ought to have the right to be preserved and not destroyed. This is an impractical sentiment, however, because beings often need to eat or molt or burn or dissolve. When I turn the ignition of my car, the engine intake valve draws a mixture of air and gasoline into the cylinder. The piston rises, compressing the mix. Once it reaches the top of its stroke, the spark plug ignites the fuel, detonating the flammable aliphatic compounds within it. The explosion drives down the piston, which in turn rotates the driveshaft. The cylinder's exhaust port opens, and the fume of exploded fuel exits toward the tailpipe. Are these gestures repugnant or reprehensible? Or are they merely thermodynamic, devoid of greater consequence?

Answers that appeal to Aristotelian final causation forget that a purpose usually implies a purpose ascribed to it *by humans*, whether directly (as in the case of the petroleum deposit that becomes a fuel) or indirectly (as in the case of the natural forest whose destruction increases biosequestration). When we talk about the ethics of internal combustion engines, we usually discuss only the first and last steps, the social and cultural practices that encourage driving in the first place, or the plume of combustion gases that exit the vehicle and enter the environment. In the first case, matters of ritual, exercise, or safety might be mustered: driving is a kind of sloth that loosens the physical and the social body alike. In the second, matters of environment take the stage: exhaust contains carbon monoxide, hydrocarbons, and particulate matter that can be harmful to living creatures.

But we don't worry much about the ethics of the spark plug, the piston, the fuel injector, or the gasoline. Does the engine have a moral imperative to explode distilled hydrocarbons? Does it do violence on them? Does it instead express ardor, the loving heat of friendship or passion? Such questions must be asked quite separately from any ethical inquiry into the processes sourcing and extracting crude oil to produce fuels and other products. They are questions not about the human imperatives for or against conservation, consumption, militarism, and related matters but about the moral relation between nonhuman, nonliving objects. "Preservation" turns out to be an object-relative concept. If a unit is a system, then objects appear, generate, collapse, and hide both within and without it with great regularity. The wind blows and then wanes, the sea ebbs and flows, the compressed fuel fills and explodes, the mineral deposit sinks and bubbles.

Take another, weirder case: theories, concepts, and memes. Is there an ethics of ideas? Not an ethics for their application, as by human hands advancing a political cause, but an ethics for the interactions of ideas as such? When I utter a phrase, does it owe more than its utterance? When it enters into relations with other utterances— whether as inscription on surface, as charge on magnetic storage devices, as disruption in the fluid dynamics of a cold morning—what responsibility do I have to it through my having uttered it? Likewise, what rights do they have relative to one another? When I encounter a catchy chorus on the radio or a clever edition of a web comic, does its desire to propagate create duty?

The microblogging service Twitter allows me to publish 140-character comments on the Internet. My "followers" receive notice of these quips, which might include links, complaints, aphorisms, or self-promotion. Like everything these days, it's a challenge to keep up with the pace of Twitter. Filled with mild malaise at this nuisance, I might lament, as I once did on the service, "Why must there be something clever to say one or more times per day?"[27] It was a sardonic outburst meant to lament the tenacity of public life today. When I don't tweet, I might lose face; my social or professional credibility could suffer. But what does such an attitude reveal if not my disregard for the ideas themselves? One of my followers responded incisively: "because your actions' continued existence might depend on it." What a thought! Why is it that one's disregard for laundry, blogs, or elliptical trainers entails only metaphorical negligence, while one's neglect of cats, vagrants, or herb gardens is allowed the full burden of genuine disregard?

Latour would describe the relations among engine parts or memes as forces between actors in a network—quasi-objects, he sometimes calls them, which are neither human nor nonhuman.[28] The forces between these objects exert transformations, Latour's replacement for relations of power. Latour helps us see the many conflicting stakeholders in a situation, all grasping for differently shaped handles to pull a network in one or another direction: "None of the actants mobilized to secure an alliance stops acting on its own behalf. They each carry on fermenting their own plots, forming their own groups, and serving other masters, wills, and functions."[29]

There is no rightful owner to whom relations return: "one form of know-how is no more 'true' than another."[30] One could respond by casting ethics as contextual, relative. This helps, to a point; I can imagine positioning myself in the context of the chickadee or the window washer. But things get murky quickly, as we move from human and animal actors to object actors: the snowblower, the persimmon, the asphalt. Is it even possible to put oneself in their shoes?

When we speak of things, are we prepared to equate their forces with their ethics? Is what a thing tends to do the same as what it considers noble or right? We might observe in an object what Aristotle calls *hexis* (ἕξις), or what Pierre Bourdieu dubs *habitus*—a way of being, a custom or routine. But a disposition is quite different from a code. Here a further problem arises, as the fact of relations shouldn't be sufficient to affirm that the actors involved in those relations act according to an ethics or in violation of one. A unit operation does not an ethics make.

When faced with pistons and soybeans, where would we look for morality? In Harman's OOO, things recede into inaccessible, private depths. When objects interact, they do so not from these depths but across their surfaces, in their sensual qualities. When fire burns cotton, it takes part only in the cotton's flammability, not in its other properties, or in its real essence, which withdraws interminably.

When we ask after the ethics of objects, we are really asking if moral qualities exist as sensual qualities. I'll float a categorical response: *no.* When the vegan eats the tofu, she bathes in its moisture, its blandness, its suppleness, its vegetality. Yet the soy does not bathe in her veganism. Through its sensual properties, she constructs a caricature of the soy, which does more than render it nutritive or gratifying; it also renders it moral. It is what Levinas calls *enjoyment*, an egoistic process for which he favors the metaphor of eating: we eat the other to make it the same.

But what of the things themselves? Does the tofu muster moral practice when slithering gently in the water of its plastic container? Does the piston when compressing air and petrol against the walls of its cylinder? Does the snowblower when its auger pulls powder from the ground and discharges it out a chute? Perhaps, although if any do, they do so through a code irrevocably decoupled from the material acts they commit. The ethics of the spark plug are no more clear to us than would be those of the vegan to the soybean plant, even as the former strips and devours the latter's salted, boiled babies in a tasty appetizer of edamame. Worse yet, there might be multiple, conflicting theories of soybean ethics—lest one assume that the noble legume is any less capable of philosophical intricacy than are bearded men.

An object enters an ethical relation when it attempts to reconcile the sensual qualities of another object vis-à-vis the former's withdrawn reality. Perhaps counterintuitively, ethics is a self-centered practice, a means of sense making necessitated by the inherent withdrawal of objects. It is a filing system for the sensual qualities of objects that maps those qualities to internal methods of caricature, a process often full of struggle. Here we find the limits of metaphorism and a good reason to respect anthropomorphism's frontier.

Can we even imagine a speculative ethics? Could an object characterize the internal struggles and codes of another, simply by tracing and reconstructing evidence for such a code by the interactions of its neighbors? It's much harder than imagining a speculative alien phenomenology, and it's easy to understand why: we can find *evidence* for our speculations on perception, like radiation tracing the black hole's event horizon, even if we are only ever able to characterize the resulting experiences as metaphors bound to human correlates. The same goes for the Foveon sensor, the piston, the tweet, and the soybean, which can only ever grasp the outside as an analogous struggle. The answer to correlationism is not the rejection of *any* correlate but the acknowledgment of *endless* ones, all self-absorbed, obsessed by givenness rather than by turpitude. The violence or ardor of piston and fuel is the human metaphorization of a phenomenon, not the ethics of an object. It is not the relationship between piston and fuel that we frame by ethics but *our* relationship to the relationship between piston and fuel. Of course, this can be productive: ethical principles can serve as a speculative characterization of object relations. But they are only metaphorisms, not true ethics of objects.

Unless we wish to adopt a strictly Aristotelian account of causality and ethics, in which patterns of behavior for a certain type can be tested externally for compliance, access to the ethics of objects will always remain out of reach. It is not the problem of objectification that must worry us, the opinion both Martin Heidegger and Levinas hold (albeit in different ways). Despite the fact that Levinas claims ethics as first philosophy, what he gives us is not really ethics but a *metaphysics of intersubjectivity* that he gives the name "ethics." And even then, Levinas's other is always another person, not another thing, like a soybean or an engine cylinder (never mind the engine cylinder's other!). Before it could be singled out amid the gaze of the other, the object-I would have to have some idea what it meant to be gazed on in the first place. Levinas approaches this position himself when he observes, "If one could possess, grasp, and know the other, it would not be other."[31] That is, so long as we don't mind only eating one flavor of otherness.

Timothy Morton observes that matters of ethics defer to an "ethereal beyond."[32] We always outsource the essence of a problem, the oil spill forgotten into the ocean, the human waste abandoned to the U-bend. Ethics seems to be a logic that lives inside of objects, inaccessible from without; it's the code that endorses expectation of plumbing or the rejoinder toward vegetarianism.

We can imagine scores of bizarro Levinases, little philosopher machines sent into the sensual interactions of objects like planetary rovers. Their mission: to characterize the internal, withdrawn subjectivities of various objects, by speculating on how object–object caricatures reflect possible codes of value and response. Object ethics, it would seem, can only ever be theorized once-removed, phenomenally, the parallel universes of private objects cradled silently in their cocoons, even while their surfaces seem to explode, devour, caress, or murder one another.

Morton offers an alternative: a *hyperobject*, one massively distributed in space-time.[33] The moment we try to arrest a thing, we turn it into a *world* with edges and boundaries. To the hammer everything looks like a nail. To the human animal, the soybean and the gasoline look inert, safe, innocuous. But to the soil, to the piston? Ethical judgment itself proves a metaphorism, an attempt to reconcile the being of one unit in terms of another. We mistake it for the object's withdrawn essence.

This confusion of the withdrawn and the sensual realms allows us to make assumptions about the bean curd and combustion engine just as we do with oceans and sewers, drawing them closer and farther from us based on how well they match our own understanding of the world. But when there is no "away," no unit outside to which we can outsource virtue or wrongdoing, ethics itself is revealed to be a hyperobject: a massive, tangled chain of objects lampooning one another through weird relation, mistaking their own essences for that of the alien objects they encounter, exploding the very idea of ethics to infinity.

DAISY CHAINS

To get at the metaphorism the sensor itself performs on a puppy the photographer frames and captures, it is necessary to speculate not only on the sensor–puppy relation from the metaphorical vantage point of the human photographer but also from the vantage point of the sensor itself. This is *metametaphorism.*

It's a scenario that extends the lesson about object ethics: metaphorisms are always self-centered. The photographer's metaphorism of the sensor can't help but draw its notes into the event horizon of human experience. Anthropocentrism is thus both a torment and a foregone conclusion for us humans, but we need not feel alone in suffering under it. If anticorrelationism amounts to a rejection of only one correlation and an embrace of multiple correlations, then centrism is inevitable—whether it be anthropocentrism, petrocentrism, photocentrism, skylocentrism, or any other. One can never entirely escape the recession into one's own centrism. A confessional is not enough. For example, when Michael Pollan mentions offhandedly that John Chapman (a.k.a. Johnny Appleseed) "had a knack for looking at the world . . . 'pomocentrically,'" he still makes an assumption of human likeness and benefit: one becomes-apple only as a means to the end of cultivation.[34]

Husserl can help. His concept of intuition exceeds sense perception to account for instincts like beneathness and justice. These *categorical intuitions* can function in what Husserl calls an "ideative" manner.[35] While Husserl intends ideative categorical intuition to allow the abstraction of the universal from the individual, we can also apply it to speculative metaphorisms of object relations disconnected from our perception of those relations, like the Foveon sensor's mesopicism or the bat's blindness. Indeed, we can even foresee such an invitation in Husserl's writing itself, as he regularly suggests that phenomenology seeks to *expand* experience.

When conceived as units—as systems of members entering and leaving configurations—aspects of the world do not disappear into an anonymous organism akin to a Latourian network or a Deleuzean assemblage. Even if these machines operate as one, they still facilitate their own breakdown into individual unit operations—the dog's sensation of the grass on its paw as it bounds across the yard, or the camera firmware's relationship to the SD card, onto which it writes data that a computer software program embedded in the camera interprets as patterns, which the device's liquid crystal display uses to produce three-color subpixel-rendered hues, which a human observer can intuit as a digital photograph. Any one of these interactions is subject to potential metaphorism—my rendition of the way the dog's paw caricatures the grass as it exerts an impression on it, or the way the Foveon sensor caricatures its view of the animal bounding across it, or of the way the LCD display caricatures the electrical signals sent to it from the device's microprocessor.

But what of the sensor's impression of the dog's impression of the grass? Or the graphics processing unit's understanding of the computer display's grasp of the signal it sends to it? Or, for that matter, the entire phenomenal chain that describes this tiny slice of existence, the one we shorthand as "taking a photograph?"

Another more extreme application of metaphorism might suture these various encounters together into a single structure. Metaphorism of this sort involves phenomenal daisy chains, built of speculations on speculations as we seep farther and farther into the weird relations between objects. The philosophical effort to bind such metaphors is nontrivial, amounting to a complex lattice of sensual object relations, each carrying an inherited yet weaker form of metaphor with which it renders its neighbor. The metaphysician who performs this task is *not* metaphorizing on *behalf* of an object down the chain—as both Nagel's account of experience and Harman's notion of withdrawal remind us, to do so would involve impossible access to a unit's own understanding of its surroundings. Instead, metaphoristic daisy chains set up nested metaphorical renderings. The relationship between the first object and the second offers the clearest rendition, insofar as a metaphor is ever really clear. The next is rendered not in terms of the second object's *own* impression of the third but as the second's *distorted* understanding of its neighbor seen through the lens of the first. It's like a tuille pastry, delicate and fragile yet discriminating and exquisite.

The metaphoristic daisy chain is a challenging structure to imagine in the abstract, yet examples of it are elusive. One candidate can be found in Ben Marcus's curious novel *The Age of Wire and String*—if indeed "novel" is an apt word for the book, whose cover describes it in different places as novel, handbook, fiction, and stories. Its contents include accounts of a world recognizable yet utterly alien, where some objects are familiar and others familiarly named, yet out of place in relation. To accommodate this curiosity, each of the book's sections is punctuated by a glossary of terms that appear within it, definitions that almost explain what has just been described while also failing utterly to do so. In the strictest sense, the book is incomprehensible.

But within that incomprehensibility, Marcus offers a webbing of object relationships that approach a metametaphoristic structure. In the chapters of the section titled "Food," one finds various explanations of apparent comestibles that nevertheless resist understanding as foodstuff. First Marcus writes that "the brother is built from food, in the manner of minute particles slowly settling or suspended by slight currents, that exist in varying amounts in all air."[36] Shortly thereafter, it becomes clear that "food-printing" is least common over the ocean compared with over cities, and that food caused by airplanes explains the heavy food-fall in Detroit. Already clues present themselves: is food meant to be precipitation, snow perhaps? For whom or what might precipitate be perceived culinarily? And what is a brother, in that case?

The next section explains "hidden food," which might be found in houses, churches, or other structures. In such situations, "artificial food (Carl) is often used to disguise the presence of real food."[37] Carl, as it happens, can be found in the chapter of terms that follows: "Name applied to food built from textiles, sticks, and rags. Implements used to aid ingestion are termed, respectively, the *lens*, the *dial*, the *knob*."[38] Soon after, other details emerge: a "food spring" can give rise to loaves of "sugar-soaked grain" or of "spore wands," which are used to pay for the right to food.[39]

Marcus's chained metaphorisms slowly slink toward a murky lucidity: Carl is a kind of food, which logic would have us conclude relates to precipitation of some sort, yet this type of food is "artificial," contained within buildings, and meant to camouflage the presence of "hidden" food. Is a phase change responsible for hiding, perhaps? What of the sticks and rags that make up Carl, which we simultaneously know to be food? What transformation has been performed on food such that textiles would now compose it? And what does it mean that this artificial food, composed of rags, would be ingested by an apparatus that bears more resemblance to a camera than a mouth (lens, dial, and knob)?

Marcus's book cannot be solved cryptographically; there is no simple chain of signifiers that the reader must simply replace in succession to produce sense. Indeed, when reading *The Age of Wire and String*, one gets the impression that sense will never emerge—not in the ordinary sense of the word, at least.

The metaphysician might read the book as a prototype for the practice of metaphoristic daisy chaining instead of as a novel. In the subjective universe of one object's perception, food is like atmospheric particles that collect and fall; in another, food hides, to be exchanged rightfully for grain loaves; in another, the artificial food that occludes the hiding fashions itself from textile and serves the interests of images.

Despite its clarity and simplicity of form and syntax, Marcus's book pushes at the very limits of human comprehension. But in doing so, it offers one possible model for daisy-chained metaphorical accounts of object perception. One metaphor clarifies a single relation, but when it becomes overloaded with the metaphor used to describe another relation its clarity clouds, resulting in distortion and confusion. Put more thematically, a metaphorism germane to its host becomes alien to the subsequent object it sequences, unable to pierce its veil and see the face of its experience.

On the first page of *A Brief History of Time*, Stephen Hawking tells the old joke of the woman who rejoins a scientist explaining the nature of the universe.

> At the end of the lecture, a little old lady at the back of the room got up and said: "What you have told us is rubbish. The world is really a flat plate supported on the back of a giant tortoise." The scientist gave a superior smile before replying, "What is the tortoise standing on?" "You're very clever, young man, very clever," said the old lady. "But it's turtles all the way down!"[40]

The story is usually meant to provoke a chuckle, an essay on both the profundity of the unmoved mover paradox and a reminder of how myth and folklore fill the gaps that science explains poorly. But Marcus's multitudinous, logically consistent yet nevertheless inscrutable accounts of food suggest we should reconsider the old lady's plea. The universe need not *literally* sit atop an infinite stack of tortoises for her statement to ring true. Rather, things render one another in infinite chains of weaker and weaker correlation, each altering and distorting the last such that its sense is rendered nonsense. It's not turtles all the way down, but metaphors.

[4]

CARPENTRY

Constructing Artifacts That Do Philosophy

As I drove home one sultry July afternoon, I listened to Tony Cox host an episode of National Public Radio's *Talk of the Nation*. The segment was titled "Writers Reveal Why They Write," a subject inspired by a *Publishers Weekly* series in which authors mused about their craft. "Writing," Cox cooed slowly in his introduction, "is a process that can be very hard work. Today, we're going to talk about writing and why we write."[1] Two guests joined the program: the memoir author Ralph Eubanks (*The House at the End of the Road*) and the short-story writer Siobhan Fallon (*You Know When the Men Are Gone*). Not best-selling authors, but successful ones, and in any event writers who had managed to get featured on a national radio program. Wasting little time, Cox got right into it. "Why do you write?" he asked of Eubanks.

"Well," began Eubanks, "I write because it's something that's really very satisfying for me. It's very gratifying." Quickly realizing that he'd never make it through the entire segment with milquetoast answers like this, Eubanks cited advice he'd received from the *Washington Post* journalist and National Book Award finalist Paul Hendrickson.

> He said first, never forget that someone asked you to tell your story. My first book, *Ever Is a Long Time* and, to a certain extent, *The House at the End of the Road* are both in the memoir genre—so [I'm] feeling very fortunate to be able to tell my story. Not very many people get an opportunity to do that.

And the other thing that he told me is that when you write, you always want to capture the cruel radiance of what is (that's a quote from Walker Evans). And he said every writer, every artist, wants to capture what is, not what you think it is but what it really is, which means you have to dig very deep into yourself and really pull out some things that are very difficult and sometimes very challenging for you.

And there's something both emotionally satisfying about it and something that is very physically satisfying when you finally see your work when it comes out in a finished book or when you see the pages at the end of the day.[2]

These are genuine if somewhat callow remarks. Gratifying though emotional satisfaction may be, surely something more must drive successful writers to write? Things didn't get much more specific when Fallon entered the conversation.

Well, all writers have that writers' adage in the back of their mind: always about writing what you know. And when I was writing this collection [*You Know When the Men Are Gone*], I was writing about the world that I was living in, which I think is sort of a unique one, and it's living on a military post and the world of or the military community. . . . I just felt like when people think military, they get this visual of an American soldier, and it's easy to sort of forget the families that all are standing behind that soldier and his mother and father and spouse or children or his, you know, if it's a female soldier, her husband. And, I don't know, I thought it was fascinating and wanted to explore that.[3]

Host and guests covered a range of other trite techniques, from carrying a notebook to record thoughts that would otherwise flit away, to the feeling of terror on seeing the blank page, to the sense of elation that comes from filling it. Overall, platitudes filled the segment: "It's like a journey, then, isn't it?" asked Cox. "I think it's being courageous and not being afraid to put something down on the page," offered Eubanks. Creative advice ought to be practical and concrete, but the host and guests of *Talk of the Nation* couldn't seem to pierce the veil on their own faces.

Mere bromide was not the problem with "Writers Reveal Why They Write." Clichés also bear truth, after all. No, the problem lies in the fact that *writing* was an arbitrary inscriptive method in the context of the show. Cox may as well have posed the question "Why do you paint?" or even "Why do you bake?" and the conversation wouldn't have changed much:

> Like, making myself sit down and forcing myself to bake is difficult, but once I get started, it's just a gorgeous feeling. It's sort of like working out. I know that's a silly analogy, but I feel like they're endorphins.[4]

The real question is subtly different: why do you write *instead of doing something else*, like filmmaking or macramé or sumi-e or welding or papercraft or gardening? Certainly particular materials afford and constrain different kinds of expression, but why should it be obvious that the choice of writing over another way of inscribing and disseminating ideas is a standard, or even desirable, one?

Natural talent may partly explain why one might choose to become a novelist instead of a musician or a painter, but talent itself—whatever indeed constitutes it—is likely unconcerned with material form. Happenstance has a greater role to play in an individual's creative fortunes. And such serendipity isn't limited to one's natural gifts; it also extends to the accident of timing. My own interest in creating and critiquing videogames, for example, is surely more a product of the circumstances in which I happen to live than it is in some inveterate natural ability to manipulate systems that themselves are mere accidents of human discovery and exploitation. Jared Diamond gets it right in his account of material history: the major events and innovations of human progress are the likely outcomes of material conditions, not the product of acute, individual genius.[5]

Still, writing is indeed a creative act recognized among many others. Even if NPR offered no insight on the matter that hot summer afternoon, we can understand intuitively that some people become writers while others become phlebotomists. However, there is one profession in which writing is not only the assumed method of creativity but practically the only one: the scholar.

For humanists, including philosophers and critics of all stripes, writing is literally the only way to scholarly productivity. One's career is measured in books and articles: publications counted on curricula vitae, citations of those publications in other written matter measured, and on and on. Smart and devoted and self-effacing though we may often be, scholars tend to overlook the unseen assumptions that underlie their professional activities.

Indeed, when philosophers and critics gather together, whether formally for conferences or by invitation for lectures, they still commit their work to writing, often reading esoteric and inscrutable prose aloud before an audience struggling to follow, heads in hands. In the humanities in particular (unlike the sciences), the academic conference is often understood as an opportunity to test out ideas in front of an audience. Those ideas will, inevitably, become professionally valid only if written down. And when published, they are printed and bound not *to be read* but merely *to have been written*. The dodgy marketing of university presses and the massive costs of journals make written scholarship increasingly inaccessible even to scholars, and publication therefore serves as professional endorsement rather than as a process by which works are made public. A few reviews earn merit enough for a positive assessment. Rinse and repeat for tenure, and again for promotion.

Even given trends in digital publishing and online distribution, including blogs and open access presses, questions about the material form of published work go unasked and unanswered. The answer is obvious: writing, always writing. Critics and philosophers will wax grandiose over Jacques Derrida's "definitive" critique of the primacy of speech over writing, writing over speech, only to insist that real scholarship is written scholarship. Is there any other kind?

But the privilege of writing isn't limited to the liberal arts. Even in science and engineering, writing casts a pallid shadow over experimentation and construction. Take the chemist who synthesizes a new polymer or the engineer who develops it into a practical and affordable building material. The results of their efforts remain invalid

PLATE 1. (a) Stephen Shore, *New York City*, 1972; (b) Stephen Shore, *Rolla, Missouri*, 1972; (c) Stephen Shore, *Room 28 Holiday Inn, Medicine Hat, Alberta*, 1974. Courtesy of the artist and 303 Gallery, New York.

PLATE 2. Stephen Shore, *Beverly Boulevard and La Brea Avenue*, 1975.
Courtesy of the artist and 303 Gallery, New York.

PLATE 3. Stephen Shore, *Perrine, Florida, November 11, 1977*.
Courtesy of the artist and 303 Gallery, New York.

PLATE 4. Stephen Shore, *Trail's End Restaurant, Kanab, Utah, August 10, 1973.*
Courtesy of the artist and 303 Gallery, New York.

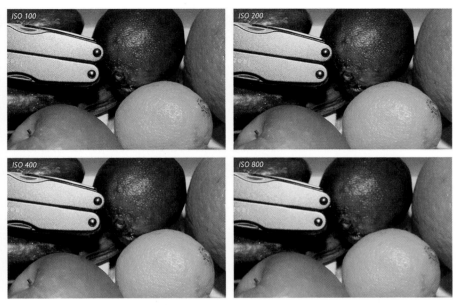

PLATE 5. As the Foveon sensor's light sensitivity is amplified, the images it records exhibit color shifts. Taking the ISO 100 image at top left as a baseline, by ISO 400 red shifts toward yellow, and green both shifts toward cyan and desaturates slightly. At ISO 800, red shifts even farther toward yellow, and green desaturates almost entirely.

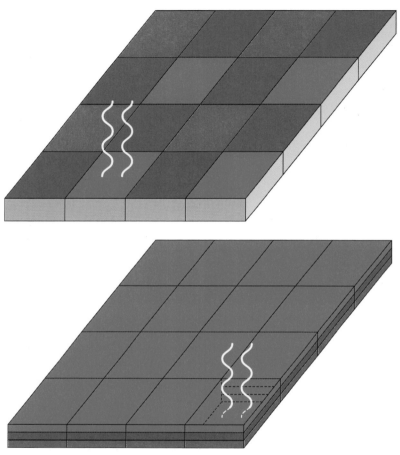

PLATE 6. A Bayer sensor *(top)* interprets colors by combining results from an array of photocells that are sensitive to a single color (red, green, or blue). In a Foveon sensor *(bottom)*, the silicon is photosensitive to different wavelengths of light at different layers of the individual photocells.

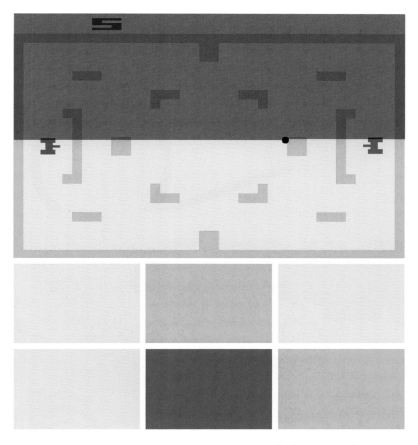

PLATE 7. *I Am TIA* is a work of carpentry that
metaphorizes the experience of an Atari television
interface adapter (TIA). At top is the reference
image, a screen from *Combat* (1977). The black dot
shows the current position of the electron gun on
the television display, the darkened area above it
having already been traversed. At bottom are six
screens sampled from the output *I Am TIA* would
display just after this moment, its internal circuitry
choosing the topmost object's color and adjusting
its signal accordingly.

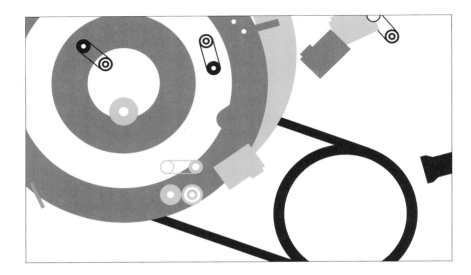

PLATE 8. Two of many possible visual states of *Tableau Machine*,
a computational "alien presence" that characterizes a home's
perception through abstract art. Reproduced courtesy of Adam Smith,
Mario Romero, Zach Pousman, and Michael Mateas.

and unaccountable until they are "written up" for publication in the proceedings of an annual field convention or a "top-tier" journal, entry into which confers the chevrons of rank on the researcher.

There's good scholarly reason to prefer the formality of written matter. The standards of quality, validity, and relevance of academic work are highly valued, and it's the job of peer review to set and uphold the bar for quality, honesty, and noteworthiness. Transparency is a virtue: findings, methods, data, and other raw materials must be made available during peer review to allow an impartial jury to assess the methods and results independently. When it goes well, this process helps ensure that scholarship maintains its Enlightenment ideal of disinterest and progress, rather than fall prey to nepotism and commercialism. These are worthwhile goals, even if contemporary peer review doesn't always embody the egalitarian rectitude to which it aspires.

An obvious question, then: must scholarly productivity take written form? Is writing the most efficient and appropriate material for judging academic work? If the answer is yes, it is so only by convention. The merit of writing as the foundation of scholarly productivity is just as arbitrary as the factors that led Eubanks and Fallon to become writers—the truth is, they (and we) did so by happenstance.

The scholar's obsession with writing creates numerous problems, but two in particular deserve attention and redress. First, academics aren't even good writers. Our tendency toward obfuscation, disconnection, jargon, and overall incomprehensibility is legendary. As the novelist James Wood puts it in his review of *The Oxford English Literary History*,

> The very thing that most matters to writers, the first question they ask of a work—is it any good?—is often largely irrelevant to university teachers. Writers are intensely interested in what might be called aesthetic success: they have to be, because in order to create something successful one must learn about other people's successful creations. To the academy, much of this value-chat looks like, and can indeed be, mere impressionism.[6]

The perturbed prose so common to philosophers, critical theorists, and literary critics offers itself up as an easy target, but it's not alone. Many scholars write poorly just to ape their heroes, thinkers whose thought evolved during the tumultuous linguistic turn of the last century.

A more prosaic and less-charged example of bad writing comes in the form of chaff: the myriad instances of "in many ways" and "could we not suggest that" and "is it not the case that" that litter academic prose. David Morris gives it the apt name "academic mumblespeak," noting how adeptly these bad habits simulate "a sentiment of precision while, at best, delaying the moment when the writer actually has to be precise."[7] Suffice it to say that academics cannot cite some deeply tended adeptness with the written word in defense of their obsession with it as a sole form of output.

Second, writing is dangerous for philosophy—and for serious scholarly practice in general. It's not because writing breaks from its origins as Plato would have it, but because writing is *only one form* of being. The long-standing assumption that we relate to the world only through language is a particularly fetid, if still bafflingly popular, opinion. But so long as we pay attention only to language, we underwrite our ignorance of everything else. Levi Bryant puts it this way:

> If it is the signifier that falls into the marked space of your distinction, you'll only ever be able to talk about talk and indicate signs and signifiers. The differences made by light bulbs, fiber optic cables, climate change, and cane toads will be invisible to you and you'll be awash in texts, believing that these things exhaust the really real.[8]

Bryant suggests that our work need not exclude signs, narrative, and discourse, but that we ought also to approach the nonsemiotic world "on its own terms as best we can."[9] Scientists and engineers may enjoy a greater opportunity to pursue extralinguistic pursuits than do humanists, but since all work inevitably pledges fealty to the written word, none are safe. When we spend all of our time reading and writing words—or plotting to do so—we miss opportunities to visit the great outdoors.

Among the consequences of semiotic obsession is an overabundant fixation on argumentation, such that pedantry replaces curiosity. Richard Rorty adeptly explains this phenomenon in his 1996 American Philosophical Association response to Marjorie Greene's *Philosophical Testament*.

> For [many philosophers] "doing philosophy" is primarily a matter of spotting weaknesses in arguments, as opposed to hoping that the next book you read will contain an imaginative, illuminating redescription of how things hang together. Many of our colleagues think that one counts as doing philosophy if one finds a flaw in an argument put forward in a philosophical book or article, and that one is a good philosopher if one is quick to find such flaws and skillful at exhibiting them.[10]

There's a fictional character in *The Simpsons* known as Comic Book Guy. Offering sarcastic quips about his favorite comics and television shows, he epitomizes the nerd-pedant who splits every last hair in his pop cultural fare. Besides serving as a send-up of the quintessential comic book/Dungeons and Dragons geek, Comic Book Guy also lampoons the nitpickery of the Internet, where everyone critiques every detail of everything all the time. But beyond those obvious references, Comic Book Guy also serves as a condemnation-by-proxy of most academics. We are insufferable pettifogs who listen or read first to find fault and only later to seek insight, if ever. "Discourse" is not a term for conversation but the brand-name for a device used to manufacture petty snipes—about the etymology of a word, or the truth value of a proposition, or the unexpected exclusion of a favorite theorist. It is perhaps no accident that among the general public, one finds behavior most similar to academic punctiliousness on the Internet, where all ideas, interchanges, and actions are strained through the sieve of language.

There is another way.

If a physician is someone who *practices* medicine, perhaps a metaphysician ought be someone who *practices* ontology. Just as one would likely not trust a doctor who had only read and written journal articles about medicine to explain the particular curiosities of one's body, so one ought not trust a metaphysician who had only read and written books about the nature of the universe. As Don Ihde puts it, "Without entering into the doing, the basic thrust and import of phenomenology is likely to be misunderstood at the least or missed at the most."[11] Yet ironically, Ihde is forced to explain such a sentiment in a book, just as I am here. What else can be done?

In his book *Shop Class as Soulcraft*, Matthew B. Crawford explains why, after earning a PhD from the University of Chicago in political philosophy, he gave up a white-collar career at a Washington think tank to become a motorcycle mechanic:

> Aristotle begins his *Metaphysics* with the observation that "all human beings by nature desire to know." I have argued that real knowledge arises through confrontations with real things. Work, then, offers a broadly available premonition of philosophy. Its value, however, does not lie solely in pointing to some more rarefied experience. Rather, in the best cases, work may itself approach the good sought in philosophy, understood as a way of life.[12]

For Crawford, knowledge and labor are not opposites but two sides of the same coin—alternatives for one another. He invites us to see that philosophy is a *practice* as much as a theory. Like mechanics, philosophers ought to get their hands dirty. Not just dirty with logic or mathematics, in the way Bertrand Russell and Alfred North Whitehead's *Principia Mathematica* investigates the logicist view of mathematics by doing mathematics, but dirty with grease and panko bread crumbs and formaldehyde. I give the name *carpentry* to this practice of constructing artifacts as a philosophical practice.

MAKING THINGS

Making things is hard. Whether it's a cabinet, a software program, or a motorcycle, simply getting something to work at the most basic level is nearly impossible. (Indeed, a great deal of Crawford's book is devoted to accounts of his challenging exploits repairing motorcycles.) Carpentry might offer a more rigorous kind of philosophical creativity, precisely because it rejects the correlationist agenda by definition, refusing to address only the human reader's ability to pass eyeballs over words and intellect over notions they contain. Sure, written matter is subject to the material constraints of the page, the printing press, the publishing company, and related matters, but those factors exert minimal force on the *content* of a written philosophy. While a few exceptions exist (Jacques Derrida's *Glas*, perhaps, or the Nietzschean aphorism, or the propositional structure of Baruch Spinoza's *Ethics* or Ludwig Wittgenstein's *Tractatus*), philosophical works generally do not perpetrate their philosophical positions through their form as books. The carpenter, by contrast, must contend with the material resistance of his or her chosen form, making the object itself become the philosophy.

Some people become writers, others jewelers, others motorcycle mechanics. Similarly, philosophical creativity can take many forms, and each philosopher's approach to carpentry will differ. In addition to increasing the variety, playfulness, and earnestness of discourse, carpentry has the added benefit of inviting thinkers to exercise and develop their natural talents in a manner akin to Heideggerian dwelling. In doing so, as Iain Thomson suggests, "we come to understand and experience entities as being richer in meaning than we are capable of doing justice to conceptually."[13]

In the context of alien phenomenology, "carpentry" borrows from two sources. First, it extends the ordinary sense of woodcraft to any material whatsoever—to do carpentry is to make anything, but to make it in earnest, with one's own hands, like a cabinetmaker. Second, it folds into this act of construction Graham Harman's philosophical sense of "the carpentry of things," an idea Harman borrowed in turn from Alphonso Lingis. Both Lingis and Harman use that phrase to refer to how things fashion one another and the world at large.[14] Blending these two notions, carpentry entails making things that explain how things make their world. Like scientific experiments and engineering prototypes, the stuffs produced by carpentry are not mere accidents, waypoints on the way to something else. Instead, they are themselves earnest entries into philosophical discourse.

Computer software is one of the things I make, so it stands to reason that my examples will come from that arena. I offer two cases of philosophical software carpentry that are particularly relevant in the present discussion, for they implement principles discussed in this book: they're ontographical tools meant to characterize the diversity of being.

When Bruno Latour composes his litanies, he does so, of course, by hand. Take a typical example:

> Try to make sense of these series: sunspots, thalwegs, antibodies, carbon spectra; fish, trimmed hedges, desert scenery; "le petit pan de mur jaune," mountain landscapes in India ink, a forest of transepts; lions that the night turns into men, mother goddesses in ivory, totems of ebony.
>
> See? We cannot reduce the number or heterogeneity of alliances in this way. *Natures* mingle with one another and with "us" so thoroughly that we cannot hope to separate them and discover clear, unique origins to their powers.[15]

This particular litany is a lovely one, full of surprising and counterintuitive units that deeply resist corroborating one another. But the lesson Latour draws from them is somewhat undermined by the manual, human nature of their selection: in some way, the nonsensical aspect of this litany is compromised by the fact that it had to be assembled by a human being. It's not enough to undermine the claim that no simple reduction can explain the objects together; nevertheless, alternative methods of demonstrating the irreduction might be philosophically desirable.

Enter the *Latour Litanizer*, a machine I constructed to produce ontographs in the form of Latour litanies. It's a simple device, but an effective one. Wikipedia, the online, user-edited encyclopedia, is built atop the wiki software platform MediaWiki. The software was originally created with Wikipedia in mind, but it has since been adapted into a general-purpose authoring and editing platform—a wiki anybody can install and use.[16] Among MediaWiki's features is a "random article" function, which pulls up a page chosen at random from the stock of articles in the wiki's database. Given Wikipedia's large number of entries—English-language articles alone number well into the millions—accessing the random article function reliably yields a page that one is unlikely to have seen before or even considered.[17]

The MediaWiki platform also offers an API, or application programming interface. An API allows a programmer to access parts of a software system's behavior from a program outside it. Some APIs are local (e.g., the APIs in an operating system like Windows or Mac OS that allow an application programmer to render user interfaces or access file management routines). Others, like the MediaWiki API, allow remote procedure calls from afar. Among the functions provided by this API is the ability to access the "random article" feature, which returns a title and a URL (among other metadata) when queried.

The *Latour Litanizer* executes queries against this API and assembles the results into a list with linked object names, one not dissimilar to the sort found in Latour's writings. Each time it's run, the *Latour Litanizer* returns a fresh, new litany. Some examples:

1949 Ostzonenmeisterschaft, Francis Levy, Hairspray (2007 film), Grammy Award for Best New Artist, Loukas Notaras, Citlalatonac, Frasier (season 3), Thallium-203, Psychology of Religion and Coping (book)

RK Jugović, Quirinius, Rozalin, Lublin Voivodeship, Christiana, Delaware

Buddha Tooth Relic Temple and Museum, Lealt Valley Diatomite Railway, Railway Protection Force Academy, Ereğli, Konya

Saint-Vincent-de-Salers, Food Lion, Dragovići, Battle of Cienfuegos, Precipitation, Sitka Pioneer Home, Alma—Marceau (Paris Métro), Thomas Mor Timotheos

Brazilian Antarctica, S. Eugene Poteat, Comiskey Park, Seneca Waterways Council, Winifred Gérin, Euchrysopsosiris, Scott C. Black, Catocala fulminea

Aidan Mitchell, Kiss Me, Baby, List of Statutory Instruments of the United Kingdom, 1951, Edson Cordeiro, Tom Webster (cartoonist), Hal Winkler, Anglican Diocese of Saldanha Bay, 2006 Wimbledon Championships—Women's Doubles

Ove, Air-Sea War—Battle (Videopac game), Augustinerkirche (Munich), Eaten Alive!, Emilio Kosterlitzky, Jetairfly destinations, Stuart Phelps, Adelaide of Holland

Argiope bruennichi, Free rider problem, Pershing LLC, Christian Reif[18]

In these lists we find people, places, organizations, ideas, fictions, groups, media, durations, and even other lists. By divorcing the author and reader from the selection process, the litanizer amplifies both the variety of types of units that exist and the variety of alliances between them. The diversity and density of tiny ontology seeps out from these litanies, both individually and (especially) when taken together.

Yet the principal virtue of the *Latour Litanizer* is also impossible to reproduce in print: the rapidness and diversity of its results. The software itself is incredibly simple to operate: a litany is loaded, and a button press calls forth another, which appears in a matter of moments. Not only does the diversity and detachment of being intensify with each fresh litany, but those very qualities also invite further exploration through the link, which leads the reader to a detailed discussion of the object in question at Wikipedia. As anyone who has ever used that website can attest, its value comes less from its ability to achieve Diderotian universal knowledge and more from its willingness to *allow anything inside,* no matter its apparent validity, relevance, or even truth value.

Consider a second, related example of simple software carpentry. In April 2010 I hosted the first OOO symposium at Georgia Tech. As a part of the preparations, I created a website to promote the event. In addition to the expected features of a conference website, such as location, speakers, abstracts, schedule, and so forth, I also constructed a visual version of the *Latour Litanizer.*[19] I had originally intended it to be little more than an evocative decoration, but it quickly proved its mettle as a philosophical device.

Unlike the litanizer, the "image toy" (I never gave it a proper name) had a more specific purpose: to illustrate the diversity of objects by demonstrating individual examples one at a time. A large portion of the website was devoted to an image of an object, and each time the page loaded, a new one would be revealed (Figure 5 offers an illustration). As a web viewer browsed through the site reading about the conference details, one small cross-section of the variety of being would unfurl.

Wikipedia is built of words, not images, so a different platform was necessary. I opted for Flickr, another user-contributed, web-based service with millions of individual entries. Furthermore, just any image wouldn't be satisfactory for the image toy to do its job.

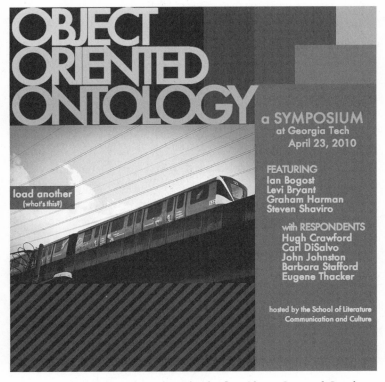

FIGURE 5. A detail from the website for the first Object Oriented Ontology symposium, held at Georgia Tech on April 23, 2010. The heavy rail transit train is one of millions of images that might appear when the page is loaded. Try it yourself at http://ooo.gatech.edu.

Many, perhaps most, images on the Flickr service depict people and scenes—the usual portraits and landscapes captured by amateur photographers. I wanted things, but things of myriad types.

When users upload images into the Flickr database, they have the option of tagging them with keywords to describe their contents. The results aren't always complete, but they offer a better account of the subject of an image than otherwise would be possible on such a large scale. Like MediaWiki, Flickr also exposes an API for external programmatic access of its databases, so my system simply needed to query for particular tags. Somewhat arbitrarily, I chose the words "object," "thing," and "stuff," discovering that these terms proved general enough to yield a wide range of different objects: a ferris wheel, a bale of hay, a railroad trellis, a circuit board, a cat, a box of files, a drainage pipe, a thatch umbrella, a lantern.

The results were aesthetically satisfactory for the purpose I had in mind. But an unexpected outcome of the image toy proved that the tool offered philosophical leverage that might have gone otherwise unseen.

The trouble started when Bryant, one of the symposium speakers, related to me that a (female) colleague had showed the site to her (female) dean—at a women's college, no less. The image that apparently popped up was a woman in a bunny suit. I never saw the image, nor did Bryant (given the millions of photos on Flickr, it's unlikely that the same one will be drawn twice), but the dean drew the conclusion that object-oriented ontology was all about objectification (I'm told that she asked why Playboy bunnies would be featured at a philosophy conference). Given the apparently objectified woman *right there on the webpage*, the impression was an understandable one, even if unintended (and certainly unsupported by OOO thought itself). Like the litanizer, the image toy includes a button to load another image, but some website viewers didn't see it, or didn't partake. By convention, website visitors expect a conference webpage to be static and to present its content in full all at once. Seeing the website as a justification of sexist objectification was an unfortunate but understandable interpretation.

Given the charged nature of the subject—a sexist "toy" on a website about an ontology conference organized by and featuring 89 percent white men—it would have been tempting to shut down the feature entirely or to eviscerate its uncertainty and replace it with a dozen carefully suggested stock images, specimens guaranteed not to ruffle feathers. But to do so would destroy the gadget's ontographical power, reducing it to but a visual flourish. Initially I resisted, changing nothing.

But, as anyone who has used the Internet knows all too well, the web is chock-full of just the sort of objectifying images exemplified by the woman in the bunny suit. Something would have to be done lest the spirit of tiny ontology risk misinterpretation. I relented, changing the search query I executed against the Flickr database:

options.Tags = "(object OR thing OR stuff) AND NOT (sexy OR woman OR girl)"

This alteration solved the problem, but as the Boolean criteria above suggest, the change also risks excluding a whole category of units from the realm of being! Are women or girls or sexiness to have no *ontological* place alongside chipmunks, lighthouses, and galoshes?

The promotional and aesthetic accomplishments of the image toy are clear enough. But its philosophical accomplishment comes from the question it poses about the challenge flat ontology and feminism pose to one another. On the one hand, being is unconcerned with issues of gender, performance, and its associated human politics; indeed, tiny ontology invites all beings to partake of the same ontological status, precisely the same fundamental position as many theorists would take on matters of identity politics. But on the other hand, the baggage of worldly stuff still exerts a political challenge on human experience that cannot be satisfactorily dismissed with the simple mantra of tiny ontology. The OOO symposium website's image toy hardly attempts to answer these questions, but it does pose them in a unique way thanks to carpentry.

It might seem silly to talk about making things as if it's a new idea. Designers, engineers, artists, and other folks make things all the time. But philosophers don't; they only make books like this one. Even Wittgenstein didn't seem to think of the famous Viennese townhouse he helped design as the practice of philosophical architecture, despite his search for a philosophy without statements and claims and arguments.

PHILOSOPHICAL LAB EQUIPMENT

Let's draw a distinction: unlike tools and art, philosophical carpentry *is built with philosophy in mind*: it may serve myriad other productive and aesthetic purposes, breaking with its origins and entering into dissemination like anything else, but it's first constructed as a theory, or an experiment, or a question—one that can be operated. Carpentry is philosophical lab equipment.[20]

Carpentry can serve a general philosophical purpose, but it presents a particularly fertile opportunity to pursue alien phenomenology. The experiences of things can be characterized only by tracing the exhaust of their effects on the surrounding world and speculating about the coupling between that black noise and the experiences internal to an object. Language is one tool we can use to describe this relationship, but it is *only* one tool, and we ought not feel limited by it.

The phenomenologist who performs carpentry creates a machine that tries to replicate the unit operation of another's experience. Like a space probe sent out to record, process, and report information, the alien phenomenologist's carpentry seeks to capture and characterize an experience it can never fully understand, offering a rendering satisfactory enough to allow the artifact's operator to gain some insight into an alien thing's experience. Again I turn to computation for examples.

Nick Montfort and I have endorsed the coupling between material constraint, creativity, and culture under the name "platform studies," a mode of analysis that explores how understanding a computer platform is vital to a critique of the particular works, genres, or categories of creative production built on top of it.[21] For example, the nature of the Atari Video Computer System's (VCS) graphics registers constrained Warren Robinett's adaptation of Willie Crowther and Don Woods's text-based *Colossal Cave* into the graphical adventure game *Adventure*, in doing so establishing the conventions of the genre. In platform studies, we shift that focus more intensely toward hardware and software as actors.

Just as the painting infects our material understanding of the photograph, so the influence of photography and cinema on television can cloud our understanding of how computers construct visual images. This confusion is understandable; after all, the television seems to be the same sort of device as that on which most computer images are displayed. It is tempting to imagine that an image like the seemingly simple combination of mazes and abstract tanks in the Atari VCS game *Combat* is drawn like a painting or a photograph. In fact, the computer's perception of its world is even less like the canvas or celluloid, let alone the human eyeball or optic nerve.

The earliest examples of computer graphics were produced on oscilloscopes, not on televisions. Like a television, an oscilloscope constructs an image by firing an electron beam at the phosphor-coated surface of the display. An oscilloscope features an electron gun that can be moved arbitrarily across the display's surface. In 1958 Willy Higginbotham created a simple tennis game he called *Tennis for Two* that uses an oscilloscope as its display. *Spacewar!*, created at MIT in 1962, employs a similar type of monitor, as does the coin-op classic *Asteroids*, although in a larger enclosure, sometimes called an XY display, a vector display, or a random-scan display. To construct an image on an XY display, the electron beam moves to a particular orientation within the tube, turns the beam on, then moves to another location, creating a line between the two with the beam's electron emissions. Each gesture must be created rapidly, before the phosphor burns off. Different phosphor qualities create different appearances on the tube's surface, and the beam's strength can sometimes be adjusted to provide more or less luminescence. From the perspective of human inscription, constructing a frame of *Asteroids* is more like drawing than like photography or cinema—or perhaps more like cuneiform inscription. But from the perspective of the evacuated glass envelope that is the monitor, it is an experience more akin to a laser light show or a rave.

An ordinary television picture of the 1970s and 1980s is displayed by a cathode ray tube (CRT). Like an oscilloscope, the CRT fires patterns of electrons at a phosphorescent screen, which glows to create the visible picture. But unlike an oscilloscope, the screen image on a television is not drawn all at once like quill on parchment but in individual scan lines, each of which is created as the electron gun passes

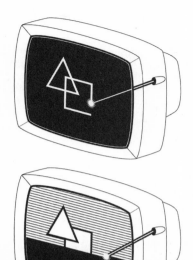

FIGURE 6. In a random-scan display (top, also known as a vector or XY display), the electron gun moves arbitrarily across the phosphorescent surface of the picture tube. In a raster-scan display (bottom), the electron beam moves from one side to another, creating an image through a series of scan lines focused through an aperture grill. A random-scan display draws its picture in a manner akin to a pencil drawing on paper, while a raster-scan display draws more like the writing in a lined notebook.

from side to side across the screen. After each line the beam turns off, and the gun resets its position at the start of the next line. It continues this process for as many scan lines as the TV image requires. Then it turns off again and resets its position at the start of the screen (see Figure 6 for a comparison).

Most modern computer systems offer a *frame buffer*, a space in memory to which the programmer can write graphics information for one entire screen. In a frame buffered graphics system, the computer's video hardware automates the process of translating the information in memory for display on the screen. But in an unusual move driven by numerous design factors, including the high cost of memory, the bare-bones television interface adapter (TIA) graphics chip in the 1977 Atari VCS makes complex seemingly basic tasks like drawing the game's screen.

The Atari does not provide services such as frame buffering for graphics rendering. The machine isn't even equipped with enough memory to store an entire screen's worth of data, just 128 bytes total. Additionally, the interface between the processor and the television is not automated, as it is in a frame-buffered graphics system. A running Atari VCS program involves an interface between ROM data, processor state, and graphics–sound interface during every moment of every line of the television display.

From a human perspective, we can render metaphorisms of the "notes" of TIA gestures. Atari VCS players see the same sorts of images that they would have come to expect from television broadcasts—the sense of a moving image like film. But the Atari VCS *itself* doesn't ever perceive an entire screen's worth of graphical data in one fell swoop. It apprehends only the syncopations of changes in registers. Its components see things still differently:

The 6502 processor encounters an instruction read sequentially from program flow, performing a lookup to execute a mathematical operation.

The TIA modulates electrical signals when its internal clock prompts it to witness a change on one of its input registers.

The RF conversion box coupled to console and television transmutes an endless stream of data into radio frequency.

Yet what do these descriptions really suggest? However appealing and familiar the usual means of doing philosophy might be, another possible method involves a more hands-on approach, manipulating or vivisecting the objects to be analyzed, mad scientist–like, in the hopes of discovering their secrets.

I created a simple artifact to attempt this feat, another example of carpentry, but this one is a tool for metaphorism. The program, which I call *I am TIA*, approximates the TIA's view of the world through the lens of a standard two-dimensional computer display. Since the TIA is synchronized to the electron gun of the television picture, instead of seeing the entire screen all at once, the TIA determines which of its objects sits atop the current position of the display and modulates its color output accordingly. Once the programmer synchronizes the game's instructions with the television's vertical blank, the TIA takes care of reading the background, playfield, and sprite patterns and colors currently set in its internal registers, converting them into a signal.

I am TIA is meant to characterize the experience of the television interface adapter, metaphorizing it for human grasp. When the program runs, it interprets screens of the videogame *Combat*, rendering only the modulated color the TIA calculates and sends to the RF adapter at a given time. Instead of seeing an entire television picture worth of image, the human operator of *I am TIA* sees only the single hue currently processed by the TIA, based on its position on the screen (Plate 7). Since the electron gun burns an entire picture into the phosphor of the television sixty times a second, the program is slowed down considerably. This rendering not only spares its human viewer seizure but also highlights the rate of chromatic experience native to the microchip, which alters its signals in time with the electron beam rather than the human eye, stopping regularly to await its position to reset to the next scan line position. In doing so, *I am TIA* also underscores part of the chip's experience that would never be graspable through human interface with the Atari: the TIA and electron beam must switch off during the television's horizontal and vertical blanks—the period when the beam resets to start a new line or a new screen.

While these moments are purely momentary in real time, when experienced through the decelerated, metaphorical lens of *I am TIA*, strange moments of black silence interrupt the characteristically bright colors of an Atari image. Time moves forward in syncopated bursts of inbound bits and bursts of signal, then of color from joystick to motherboard to television. Despite the fact that the machine must manually synchronize itself to the television display at 60 Hz, it has no concept of a screen's worth of image. It perceives only a miasma of instruction, data, color, darkness.

Other works of alien phenomenal carpentry exist, too, even if they don't explicitly frame themselves in that way. Consider Ben Fry's *Deconstructulator*.[22] The program is a modification of a Nintendo Entertainment System (NES) emulator, which runs any NES ROM as if it were being played on the original hardware. On the periphery, the system depicts the current state of the machine's sprite memory in ROM, sprite data in video memory, and current palette registers, which are mapped via keys to the indexed values in the sprites themselves (Figure 7). These update over time as the state of the machine changes while the user plays. While *I am TIA* metaphorizes only one component of the Atari VCS console, *Deconstructula-*

tor offers an operational, exploded view of the entire NES memory architecture, particularly its sprite and palette systems. From a carpenter's perspective, the result opens the hidden file drawers of the NES cartridge, depicting its contents and revealing how the machine manipulates the game's contents within the limitations of its memory constraints.

Even without the fancy packaging of *Deconstructulator*, source code itself often offers inroads in alien phenomenology—particularly when carpentered to reveal the internal experiences of withdrawn units. *Firebug* is a Firefox web browser plug-in that allows the programmer or ordinary user to monitor and display the internal states of the web browser's rendering and behavior system as a page is displayed.[23] Once installed, the tool allows a user to view the HTML that corresponds with a selected visual element on the screen, to reveal and modify the style information (or CSS) that tells the browser which colors, fonts, layout styles, and positions to use for objects on the page, to overlay rectilinear grids to reveal the internal metrics of

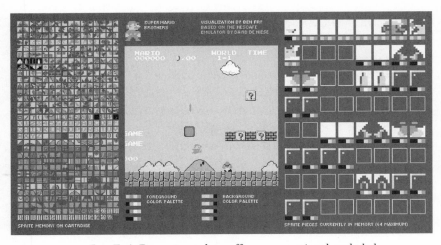

FIGURE 7. Ben Fry's *Deconstructulator* offers an operational exploded view of the Nintendo Entertainment System. In this image, sprite memory appears on the left. Color sets, half a byte in size, colorize the sprites— the active sets appear below the *Super Mario Bros.* screen. At right, the machine's current memory configuration is displayed, including all the sprites and their associated color sets.

a webpage, to review the network activity and duration required to fetch and retrieve every object needed for the page, to debug scripts and show the runtime values of active variables, to reveal the internal object structure of the page within the document object model (DOM) used for both stylesheet rendering and scripted behavior, and so forth.

ALIEN PROBES

But a much more sustained and deliberate example of computational carpentry that performs alien phenomenology can be found in *Tableau Machine*, a nonhuman social actor created by Mario Romero, Zachary Pousman, and Michael Mateas. In 1998 researchers at Georgia Tech began constructing an "Aware Home," a real residence just north of campus that was outfitted with devices, screens, interfaces, cameras, and sensors. Its initial investigators posed the question, "Is it possible to create a home environment that is aware of its occupants' whereabouts and activities?" It's an inquiry with an assumption: that the only thing a home can do is to serve its human occupants.[24] As Romero and colleagues put it, research in ubiquitous computing and ambient intelligence "remains rooted in an information access and task-support where the goal is long term active reflection on everyday activity, enjoyment and pleasure."[25] In response to this limitation, Romero, Pousman, and Mateas propose an "alien presence," a computational agent that senses and interprets the state of an environment (in this case a home) and reports its experience in the form of abstract art. An alien presence, they argue, "does not try to mimic human perception and interpretation, but rather to open a non-human, alien perspective onto everyday activity."[26]

Tableau Machine attempts to represent the perceptual apparatus of the entire house by harnessing the Aware Home's array of cameras, divided into regions, and interpreting the changing images with computer vision algorithms that measure motion in those regions. Instead of predicting or encouraging particular behaviors on the part of individual human actors in the home, as other ubiquitous computing efforts have attempted, *Tableau Machine*'s system interpolates the accumulation and release of motion, which its creators characterize as social energy, social density, and social flow.[27] And rather than depict this information in a one-to-one fashion meant for human legibility, as an information visualization might do, *Tableau Machine* renders the home's perception as an occasionally changing work of abstract art shown on a plasma display mounted in the home (as if it were a painting or television). The images that appear on that screen follow the general style of fauvism or postimpressionism, but they do not attempt to simulate the style of any particular artist or artistic movement (see Plates 8a and 8b for examples).

Tableau Machine takes for granted that the home *itself* is a unit, one distinct from but inclusive of its kitchen, living room, dining room, and hallways. Its creators surmise that the home can perceive, but they add an additional presumption: a home's perception is unfathomable by its human occupants. Instead of understanding it, the best we can do is trace the edges of its dark noise, producing a caricature of its experience in a form we can recognize. In *Tableau Machine*'s case, the rendition is *literally* caricature, that of abstract art.

Tableau Machine does not try to improve the function of the home or the providence of its occupants. Instead, it hopes only "to encourage engaging conversations and reflections by opening unusual viewpoints into everyday life."[28] That said, Romero, Pousman, and Mateas don't take *Tableau Machine* as far into the great outdoors as they might, conceding that it "characterizes human activity."[29] The project's context may help explain that misstep; after all, the three documented the project for publication in the prestigious proceedings of the Association of Computing Machinery Computer-Human Interaction conference (yet another example of the predominance of writing in scholarship, even when the scholarly object is an apparatus). Human–Computer Interaction (HCI) concerns itself with *human*-computer relations, not computer-computer relations — or house-computer relations, for that matter. Despite its technical tenor, computing is just as correlationist a field as everything else, obsessed with human goals and experiences.

When allowed to break free of this context, it's clear that *Tableau Machine* is something quite different: it's an alien probe that turns *us* into the aliens, gathering data from a strange visual field, analyzing it according to a curious and unfathomable internal logic, and reporting back its distorted impressions of our extraterrestrial world, just as a robotic space probe might collect radio signals, process radiation signatures, and present an earnest yet inevitably erroneous account of life in the universe.

A field study conducted by *Tableau Machine*'s creators proves the point. They installed the object in three homes in the Atlanta area, effectively transforming the residences of ordinary families into cyborg homes. *Tableau Machine* remained for six to eight weeks in each house, during which time the occupants reported engaging deeply with the curious artifact. Some of these observations were more about engineering than about perception, such as discovering through experimentation that the same domestic states would never generate precisely the same abstract images.[30] But others saw the abstract images *Tableau Machine* produced as interpretations of the way their respective homes perceive:

> Near the beginning of the deployment, B2 (the mother) began to describe images as being views of the house, either from above or from other perspectives. Other householders followed along in this reasoning, and pointed out clusters that were "the kitchen table" or "the hallway." As the deployment progressed, B householders began to see individuals in the images, and to draw parallels between activities (such as a boisterous dinner) and the images (a large round shape full of messy shapes on top, including a set of lines that formed something resembling a fork). The family was quite enamored with this image, and others that represented moments around the house. In the last week, Betty found an image that looked like a smiling face, which she took (or pretended to take) as an image of her husband cooking at the stove. At the interview she was very proud of the printout and asked if she could keep it. She hung this picture on the refrigerator.[31]

To be sure, this and other impressions of *Tableau Machine* clearly reveal attempts at anthropomorphism on the part of the family. But as Jane Bennett predicts, such an attitude helps deliver the home's residents out of anthropocentrism.[32] While the mother remains concerned about the members of her family, their activities, and their welfare, her experience of domesticity is nevertheless expanded, such that the perception of the house itself has become a part of her sympathies.

Latour Litanizer, I am TIA, Deconstructulator, Firebug, and *Tableau Machine* are *artifacts* of alien phenomenology. Rudimentary perhaps, but concrete, unburdened by theoretical affectation. These examples show how speculation might be used in an applied fashion. They also show that the job of the alien phenomenologist might have as much or more to do with experimentation and construction as it does with writing or speaking. One form of carpentry involves constructing artifacts that illustrate the perspectives of objects.

The relationships between memory addresses and ROM data, or webpages and markup, or households and electronic paintings offer but a few examples of the object perceptions carpentry can reveal. For other things also take place at this very moment, adding themselves and their kindred to the volcanoes, hookahs, muskets, gearshifts, gypsum, and soups that have arisen. Here are some that interest me, but yours will surely vary:

An electron strikes phosphor, lighting a speck on a fluorescent tube that glows and fades.

A metal catch closes a circuit on silicon, whose state a processor bitwise compares to a charge on another wafer.

An I/O bus pushes an OpenGL instruction into the onboard memory of a video card, whose GPU runs matrix operations into the video memory soldered to its board.

Carpentry's implications for weird realism in general might be even more surprising: the philosopher-programmer is joined by the philosopher-geologist, the philosopher-chef, the philosopher-astronomer, the philosopher-mechanic. The "carpentry of things," one of Harman's synonyms for object-oriented philosophy, might be a job description, not just a metaphor.

A NEW RADICALISM

In a discussion of Whitehead's take on creativity, Steven Meyer reminds us that the former's writing shares a quality with poetry: "In inventing creativity, Whitehead was doing what poets are best known for doing: naming things that do not already have names, or—what comes to the same thing—giving a new name to something and thereby transforming it."[33] Meyer also reminds us of one of Whitehead's famous aphorisms, the kind that makes him the most quoted and the least cited of philosophers: "In the real world it is more important that a proposition be interesting than that it be true."[34]

Latour offers his own version of this injunction: "Standing by what is written on a sheet of paper alone is a risky trade. However this trade is no more miraculous than that of the painter, the seaman, the tightrope walker, or the banker."[35] Knowledge, he concludes, "does not exist. . . . Despite all claims to the contrary, crafts hold the key to knowledge."[36]

Yet once we are done nodding earnestly at Whitehead and Latour, what do we do? We return to our libraries and our word processors. We refine our diction and insert more endnotes. We apply "rigor," the scholarly version of Tinker Bell's fairy dust, in adequate quantities to stave off interest while cheating death. For too long, being "radical" in philosophy has meant writing and talking incessantly, theorizing ideas so big that they can never be concretized but only marked with threatening definite articles ("the political," "the other," "the neighbor," "the animal"). For too long, philosophers have spun waste like a goldfish's sphincter, rather than spinning yarn like a charka. Whether or not the *real* radical philosophers march or protest or run for office in addition to writing inscrutable tomes—this is a question we can, perhaps, leave aside. Real radicals, we might conclude, *make things*. Examples aren't hard to find, and some even come from scholars who might be willing to call themselves philosophers.

Meanwhile once more, at the Genoa-based brand consultancy Urustar, designers recast and condense hundreds of pages of my books into playable pixel art.[37]

Meanwhile, at NYU, Alex Galloway implements a computer version of Guy Debord's *Le Jeu de la Guerre*, revealing in the process that Debord and his partner Alice Becker Ho misapplied their own rules in their book about the game.[38]

Meanwhile, at Fergus Henderson's London restaurant St. John, the chef practices philosophy of "nose to tail eating," rescuing neglected cuts of meat and offal for innovative preparations.[39]

Meanwhile, in the courtyard of the Skiles classroom on the Georgia Tech campus, my colleague Hugh Crawford directs his Special Topics in Literature and Culture class in the construction of a full-size wooden hut as a part of their study of Henry David Thoreau's *Walden*.[40]

These examples do more than put theory into practice; they also represent practice *as* theory. It's not that writing cannot be interesting. Rather, we might consider that writing *is not the only* method of engendering interest.

If we take vicarious causation seriously, if we believe that things never really interact with one another, but only fuse or connect in a locally conceptual fashion, then the only access any object has to any other is conceptual. When people or toothbrushes or siroccos make sense of encountered objects, they do so through metaphor. As Whitehead and Latour suggest, this process requires creative effort, challenging OOO to become craftsmanship, challenging us to learn a trade. We tend to think of creativity as construction, the assembly of something new out of known parts. A novel is made of words and ink and paper, a painting of pigments and canvas and medium, a philosophy of maxims and arguments and evidence, a house of studs and sheetrock and pipes. Perhaps in the future, following Crawford's example, radical philosophers will raise not their fists but their hammers.

[5]

WONDER

In his blog-turned-best-selling-humor-book *Stuff White People Like*, Christian Lander explains that, whenever possible, white people prefer not to own a television. They do so, says Lander, precisely so they can report indignantly about their refusal to own a set when water cooler conversation turns to last night's *Lost* or *American Idol*.[1]

Despite the white person's natural aversion to television—and here it is probably important to clarify that when Lander says "white people," he really means the liberal, upper-middle-class, latté-swilling, Volvo-driving variety—there is one type of program they do like, the kind that is "critically acclaimed, low-rated, shown on premium cable, and available as a DVD box set."[2] The apotheosis of such programming, suggests Lander, is *The Wire*, David Simon's five-series, sixty-episode survey of the Baltimore drug scene, as seen through the eyes of its participants: dealers, politicians, kingpins, junkies, public defenders, and cops. Here's how Lander summarizes *The Wire*'s role in contemporary culture, writing on the eve of the show's series finale in 2008:

> For the past three years, whenever you say "*The Wire*" white people are required to respond by saying "it's the best show on television." Try it the next time you see a white person! Though now they might say "it *was* the best show on television.
>
> So why do they love it so much? It all comes down to authenticity. A long time ago, someone started a rumor that when *The Wire* is on TV, actual police wires go quiet because all the dealers are watching the show. Though this is not true,

it seems plausible enough to white people and has imbued the show with the needed authenticity to be deemed acceptable.[3]

The Wire isn't alone. Shows like *The Sopranos, Mad Men,* or New Mexico's own drug drama, *Breaking Bad,* offer just the right measure of what we casually, infuriatingly call "human experience." You can almost hear it: the critic, the scholar, the latté-swiller writing, speaking, or (even better) blogging about how *The Wire* or *Mad Men* offers "an incisive exploration of the murky depths of human experience." Michel Foucault, Jacques Lacan, and Gilles Deleuze might make an appearance, serving their role as the mirepoix of high-culture criticism. It doesn't make it into Lander's blog or book, but we might as well add *critical theory* as another page in his informal sociology.

Lander and Lacan notwithstanding, the appeal of TV shows like *The Wire* comes from their ability to "tell us something about ourselves," to use another critical shorthand that has somehow risen above its inherent triteness. Midgrade dealer D'Angelo Barksdale, detective James McNulty, kingpin Avon Barksdale, police lieutenant Cedric Daniels, stevedore Frank Sobotka, mayoral hopeful Tommy Carcetti, newspaper editor Gus Haynes: these are the objects of concern for the drug scene. These are the actants that form the network of its operation. Yet despite the show's rhetoric of inclusiveness and complexity, others are summarily ignored: the Maryland Transit Authority bus that trundles through the Broadway East neighborhood; the synthetic morphine derivative diacetylmorphine hydrochloride, which forms the type of heroin powder addicts freebase; Colt .45 (the firearm), and Colt 45 (the malt liquor).

COMPETING REALISMS

When people (white or otherwise) talk about *The Wire,* they discuss it as an example of realism. Here *realism* means two things, both quite different from the philosophical realism the new speculativism embraces.

First, it suggests the truthful, or round, or otherwise complex characters that make the show rise above its presumably vapid brethren. The "authenticity" of the show's dealers, cops, longshoreman, city councilmen, middle-school students, and journalists is established through a set of cinematic rhetorics, including their anonymity as actors, their racial diversity, their ordinary appearance, and, perhaps most importantly, the almost impossibly inscrutable intricacy of their actions and relations, a feature that makes television "smart" in a Steven Johnson, *Everything Bad Is Good For You* sort of way.

Second, it silently clarifies the type of realism at work in the series: this is not the ontological realism of process philosophy or science or even transcendentalism but the representational realism of cinema and photography. *Social realism* we usually call it, following the influence of such writers as Charles Dickens and Thomas Hardy, such artists as Reginald Marsh and Walker Evans, and such filmmakers as Tony Richardson and Mike Leigh. By definition, social realism adopts the nature–culture split that Bruno Latour critiques in *We Have Never Been Modern*, the cultural aspects of reality enjoying relief against the background domain of nature.

As a creative work, *The Wire* is thus incapable of giving its viewers any sensation of the constituent parts of its subject (Baltimore), *unless* those parts are mediated by the actions of its human agents. Part of the problem is philosophical: Simon's creative progression from journalist to screenwriter makes correlationism an inevitability. He is in the business of telling *people's* stories. But another part may be material: can we even imagine a dramatic serial that delves deeply into the compression heat of a diesel engine combustion chamber, or the manner by which corn or sugar additives increase the alcoholic content of malt, or the dissolution of heroin in water atop the concave surface of a spoon, as *The Wire* does for the social and psychological motivations of junkies and drug dealers? Even at best, the result might resemble a *Saturday Night Live* sketch gone wrong: 3-2-1 *Contract* or *Mutual of Omaha's Wild Kingpin*.

In *Stuff White People Like*, Lander suggests *American Idol* as a natural inverse of *The Wire*, a show whose empty spectacle infuriates the Patagonia set. But if it's a deeper respect for all objects within a domain that we're after, then I'd suggest an alternate antithesis. It's another cable network show, and it also takes place in Baltimore, and it also deals with the rough-and-tumble, tenuous relationships between the complex constituent parts of structures that otherwise recede into the background, oblivious.

I'm referring, of course, to *Ace of Cakes.*

The show tracks baker Duff Goldman, whose shop Charm City Cakes sits right smack in the middle of the blighted neighborhoods of Oliver and Greenmount West where *The Wire* takes place. Two-tenths of a mile up North Gay Street from Duff's bakery sits the abandoned American Brewery; an overgrown lot behind it serves as a frequent location for drug deals in *The Wire.*[4] Walk the same distance in the other direction, and you'll reach the stretch of Bethel Street between Federal and Oliver that bears the cinderblock wall graffito "Bodymore, Murdaland," an image that graces the show's opening credits.

It's an area that has enjoyed some reversal of fortune in recent years, the urban decay that followed the Baltimore riot of 1968 having been partly, slowly replaced by redeveloped rowhouses and bohemian artist culture. And unlike "Bodymore," "Charm City" is one of Baltimore's official nicknames. Duff's adoption of the name for a specialty bakery so close to the heart of Simon's fictionalized drug-addled Murdaland provides an overflowing spoonful of ironic juxtaposition.

Inside the bakery, Duff wields another kind of white powder—to make cakes. Custom cakes, the kind that might be shaped like a swamp boat or topped with a family of sculpted candy burrow owls. As with all reality programming, a good deal of personality and dispute drives the show's narrative flow. In *Ace of Cakes*'s case, schedules and mishaps usually provide the drama, with many more cake orders coming in than seem reasonable to complete in the week, and with material experiments in fondant, cake, and dowel resulting in inevitable structural integrity challenges. In the end, of course, the cakes always go out and the customers are always awestruck at the fruit of Duff and crew's labor. At a minimum rate of $1,000 per cake, it might be a more profitable racket than the heroin trade down the block.

The Wire tries to take apart the institutional complexities of bureaucratic experience. It draws from every aspect of every variety of human motivation and behavior, and in doing so it delivers a subtle, harrowing critique of the fine line between the tragic and the banal. Things go wrong slowly, with a whimper. *Ace of Cakes* does the opposite: it deletes human rationales as much as possible, forcing birthdays and weddings and retirements to serve as mere stages for the more interesting and important process of cake construction.

In one episode, Duff's crew constructs a cake in the form of the *Gokstad*, a ninth-century Viking ship named for the farm in Norway where it was excavated in 1880.[5] It had been commissioned as a wedding cake for two Viking reenactors, who planned their wedding as a part of a weeklong Viking festival. The couple's story offers some necessary setup, but from there the ship and cake themselves take center stage, and the show offers a systematic examination of the construction of both.

The *Gokstad* was a warship, fashioned of oak through clinker building, a method of assembly in which planks overlap and connect at their tops along an overlapping joint. After a frame is assembled, the battens of oak would have been steam-bent to fit the ship's internal shape. Joints called *lands* were fashioned through *joggling*, the cutting of triangular recesses into the frame to secure a fit for the planks. At twenty-three meters long, the *Gokstad* is the largest vessel on display at the Viking Ship Museum in Oslo, in fact. It boasts steerage access for thirty-two oarsmen, although wooden disks would have been secured in the holes to protect the men in battle and to keep out water.

While Charm City's cake version of the *Gokstad* doesn't mirror the shipbuilding techniques of the Viking Age, the end product is a convincing replica, complete with hull, oars, oar covers, mast, and sail. The hull itself was carved from layered, frosting-bound cake, but the clinker planking was applied via strips of fondant or buttercream, which were then frosted to match the appearance of oak.

To satisfy the viewer's expectation for human drama, the Charm City staff drives the cake to Ohio, where the baked *Gokstad* is revealed to its would-be warrior captains amid the weird mirth of the festival. But the couple, who must have paid thousands for the end product, miss out on witnessing its creation. Eating relegates the cake to its purportedly rightful place as ceremonial foodstuff, but the rest of the show flattens the ontological seas, as it were. Clinker-built oak planks and fondant, keel, hull, and sponge cake, white-topped waves and spread frosting, oar stay and cookie all take their places next to each other as objects of equivalent existence. But more so, the television production itself reveals each component to have equal potential interest *on its own terms.* Clinker planks yield as much fascination as do completed warships. The layers of frosted cake that form the firmament of hull once carved from rectangular blocks prove no less endearing than the candy-molded oars or the tar sealant that would have waterproofed the original *Gokstad.*

Duff adds to the valid stuffs of baking by introducing techniques from carpentry, sculpture, and the plastic arts; power tools are regularly featured in episodes of *Ace of Cakes,* for example, to rough out the supporting frame and stand for a Millennium Falcon cake. Here, too, no object remains less motivating than any other: every pipe, window, and exhaust vent finding its place alongside cockpit, Wookiee, or indeed the very *Star Wars* universe in which these objects find fictional resonance.

But if Simon errs in revealing only the human aspects of his subject, Duff errs in offering only a tiny morsel of the rich ontological underbelly of his creations. If it's the food itself we're hungry for, we'll have to hold out for another former Food Network staple, Alton Brown's *Good Eats.*

Some compare Brown's approach with that of the science educators Mr. Wizard or Bill Nye, because Brown's show explores the science and technology of food with special attention paid to the chemical processes at work in cooking and the technical ups and downs of different equipment. While Brown doesn't limit himself to sweets like Duff, he has featured cake baking on the show. His technique adds a different layer to the realisms one can watch on television.

Alton's Good Eats Pound Cake offers not only a (presumably) tasty treat but also a set of insights into the entities and processes that constitute it. For example, when constructing a batter, it's common to use the "creaming method," an approach to ingredient mixing that is said to increase the lightness and tenderness of the resulting cake. Put simply, it goes like this:

1. Beat fats
2. Beat sugar with fat
3. Add eggs
4. Alternately add dry and wet ingredients

The first two steps produce tiny air bubbles in the batter. The greater these are in consistency and number, the lighter and fluffier the resulting cake will bake. As for the dry ingredients (usually flour, baking soda, and salt), if these are mixed together evenly in advance, then the salt and leavener disperse evenly throughout the batter, which will in turn allow it to rise more evenly when baked. Ever the kitchen gadget geek, Alton recommends a heavy stand mixer for the best distribution. His even has flame decals on the sides.

Most creaming method instructions offer vague advice, like "beat butter until light and fluffy." But what exactly counts as light and fluffy? Here's where Brown's method is unique; for every situation of this kind, he has an approach. In this case, the abstraction "light and fluffiness" gets its own unit operation:

> Okay, there I go using those vague terms of "light" and "fluffy." Here's when to stop: when you're no longer able to see sugar granules, but you can still feel them if you rub a bit of the creamed fat between your fingers. Although you can overcream (and you'll know that you have when your mixture moves from a smooth and homogeneous mixture to something akin to curdled milk), inadequate aeration (i.e. under-creaming) is far more common. As a rule of thumb, I like to see the volume of the fat increase by a third.[6]

Brown's other tips likewise identify the unseen stuff of cookery. For one, he suggests mixing the eggs separately, rather than adding them one at a time to the mix (as most recipes call for). Doing so emulsifies the water-heavy egg whites with the yolks, reducing the amount of liquid introduced into the fats. The type of fat makes a difference, too. Alton recommends slow-churned European-style butters, because their smaller butterfat crystals produce smaller bubbles and therefore a finer texture in the cake. And while you're at it, opt for cake flour over all-purpose flour. The finer flour particle size, lower protein level, and bleaching all serve to tenderize and normalize the cake's final texture.

Brown's cakery embraces tiny ontology. The cake exists, to be sure. So does the Kitchen-Aid 5-Quart Stand Mixer, the preheated oven, the mixing bowl, and the awaiting gullet. But so too do the sugars, the flour granules, the butterfat crystals, the leavener, the gas bubbles. And they do not merely *exist*—they exist *equally,* and *Good Eats* proves that flat existence entails *equal levels of potential worth.* The relationship between fat crystal and sugar, leavener and batter is just as fundamental as that between cake and mouth. The dispersion of gases that rises is surely interesting and useful as it relates to the end product (a light and fluffy cake), but *Good Eats* also presents the gas bubbles and the flour granules as *their own* end product, worthy of consideration, scrutiny, and even awe.

AWE

Awe is a weird notion in philosophy. It might not be first found in Plato, but it is there that it finds one of its two most famous mentions. In the dialogue *Theaetetus,* Socrates recounts a conversation with the young orphan who gives the piece its title. Theodorus had recommended his student Theaetetus to Socrates as a promising pupil, and furthermore one who rather resembles Socrates (the dialogue would lead us to believe that this is not a compliment).

Socrates asks Theaetetus to help him figure out what knowledge is. The young man, who had just finished rubbing himself down with oil, is caught somewhat by surprise as he passes the two old men with newly anointed friends. He responds that he has no idea how to answer such a question, but (of course) Socrates persists. Theaetetus musters a salvo, submitting that knowledge is just perception.

As is common with Socratic interlocutors, Theaetetus is now stuck, his mentor Theodorus having committed him to more than a passing hello, as it turns out. Socrates recounts ad nauseam a litany of logical fallacies, a review of Homer, a detour through *Protagoras,* not to mention the extensive digression about midwifery Socrates incants as a way to persuade Theaetetus that the latter did indeed have a definition of knowledge seeking exit from his brain, like a newborn from a womb.

After going through a great many puzzles meant to trace the edges of knowledge, Theaetetus admits, "No, indeed, it is extraordinary how they set me wondering whatever they can mean. Sometimes I get quite dizzy with thinking of them."[7] Socrates responds with what will become an oft-quoted quip:

That shows that Theodorus was not wrong in his estimate of your nature. The sense of wonder is the mark of the philosopher. Philosophy indeed has no other origin, and he was a good genealogist who made Iris the daughter of Thaumas.[8]

In Greek mythology, Iris is the messenger who couples earth and the heavens, connecting humanity to the gods. As for the bit about genealogy, Socrates is referring to Hesiod, who explains that Iris was the daughter of the sea god Thaumas and Electra, an air nymph. Iris is also the goddess of the rainbow, which connects earth and heaven through air.

But this digression about Iris and Thaumas makes sense only in Greek: the word Theaetetus uses in his admission of dizziness is θαυμάζω, I wonder. The name of Thaumas the god (Θαῦμας) is also the word for wonder (θαῦμα).

Wonder has two senses. For one, it can suggest awe or marvel, the kind one might experience in worship or astonishment. But for another, it can mean puzzlement or logical perplexity. From a philosophical perspective, it is tempting to conclude that the second meaning is what Socrates and Plato have in mind: philosophy as a process of reason, through which the mysterious is brought down to earth, like the work of Iris. This is certainly how most philosophers have understood Socrates's wonder—particularly when it is read through Aristotle, who more explicitly argues that wonder catalyzes understanding.[9]

But there is another way to understand these two meanings in the context of Theaetetus, particularly since the dialogue ends without resolution, its interlocutors satisfied to conclude that they have been reminded of the need to have humility about the knowledge they do not possess. When seen in this way, the rainbow daughter of wonder offers not just a road that allows traversal between earth and heaven but also one that demands pause for its own sake. This is not one of those irreconcilable Derridean suspensions, either. It's a truly simultaneous condition without deferral.

Let's keep the rainbow road analogy for a moment: I once traversed the Hana highway, which runs across the lush, windward side of Maui between Kahului and Hana, then continues across the island's dry, volcanic south edge, around the Haleakala Crater. It's a tourist destination unto itself (and far more so than the sleepy town of Hana that is its apparent destination). The average speed on this road is fifteen miles per hour, not by regulation but because its winding curves, narrow passes, and numerous overhangs, bridges, and waterfalls demand slowness. Yet this narrow, winding road is also the only means of passage by land from the business and transit center of Maui to the town of Hana.

This is a subtly different case than the "scenic route," which offers an aesthetically appealing but more indirect path from place to place. It's true, for example, that traveling the beachfront Pacific Coast Highway between Los Angeles and San Francisco offers a picturesque alternative to Interstate 5, whose most memorable feature is the stench of industrial cattle slaughterhouses between Coalinga and Los Baños. But driving the PCH also adds at least an hour and a half to the travel time.

The Hana highway is both route and destination, like the object of philosophy is both puzzle to be decoded and object to be admired. Likewise, the leavener's gasses can excite the passions as much as can the cake they cause to rise. The fondant planks deserve ceremony as much as the wedding their mock Gokstad punctuates, the heroin spoon demands as much intrigue as the institutional dysfunctions that intersect it.

A second well-known appearance of wonder comes from Francis Bacon, who extends Aristotle's catalyzing wonder through two metaphors. Wonder, says Bacon, is both "the seed of knowledge" and also "broken knowledge."[10] The first of these accounts is more or less identical to Aristotle's version. But the latter is more complex. Bacon calls admiration (*admiratio*, Latin for wonder) "that which maintains a distance," as in the case of the necessary distance from knowledge of God. The eighteenth-century philosopher, diplomat, and monarchist Joseph-Marie de Maistre suggests, "without the least doubt," that Bacon's concept is best understood as "a science attached to nothing" or "a knowledge without knowledge."[11] While our wonder can be transformed partly into knowledge, for Bacon the road toward knowledge of creation itself remains impassible. The embrace of this brokenness partly explains Bacon's interest in the aphorism, which executes a performance of discontinuity, like rocks blocking Iris's highway. Maistre explains confidently:

> As for the proof that one would like to draw from the idea of God, it is permitted to regard it as a veritable joke, since we can have NO IDEA of God. *There remains the Bible,* which makes man a theist, as a serinette makes a bird a musician.[12]

Knowledge may intersect or surround ideas and objects, but it never permeates them, just as a mechanical device used to train canaries doesn't really turn them into sopranos. Understood in this way, wonder would seem to be quite the opposite of its earlier Aristotelian catalyst. Bacon likens it to arrest, incapacity:

> Wonder causeth astonishment, or an immoveable posture of the body; casting up of the eyes to heaven, and lifting up of the hands. For astonishment, it is caused by the fixing of the mind upon one object of cogitation, whereby it doth not spatiate and transcur, as it useth; for in wonder the spirits fly not, as in fear; but only settle, and are made less apt to move. As for the casting up of the eyes, and the lifting up of the hands, it is a kind of appeal to the Deity, which is the author, by power and providence, of strange wonders.[13]

A fundamental separation between objects is fundamental to OOO, and in that light we might wish to fuse Bacon's and Plato's accounts of wonder while secularizing them from both their pagan and Judeo-Christian contexts. In each case, things become suggestive of knowledge, with some sort of puzzlement initiating a drive toward investigation. But, simultaneously, the Platonic, Aristotelian, and Baconian concepts of wonder also underscore the irreconcilable separations between all objects, chasms we have no desire or hope of bridging—not by way of philosophy, not through theism, not thanks to science. Knowledge doesn't remain out of reach, as Socrates and Bacon would have it, but rather the very pursuit of that knowledge is metaphysically undesirable.

Maistre's quip about a "science attached to nothing" is thus more than mere provocation. The act of wonder invites a detachment from ordinary logics, of which human logics are but one example. This is a necessary act in the method of alien phenomenology. As Howard Parsons puts it, wonder "suggests a breach in the membrane of awareness, a sudden opening in a man's system of established and expected meanings."[14] To wonder is to suspend all trust in one's own logics, be they religion, science, philosophy, custom, or opinion, and to become subsumed entirely in the uniqueness of an object's native logics—flour granule, firearm, civil justice system, longship, fondant.

In Graham Harman's terms, wonder is a sort of *allure* that real objects use to call at one another through enticement and absorption. As he puts it, "Allure merely alludes to the object without making its inner life directly present."[15] Wonder describes the particular attitude of allure that can exist between an object and the very concept of objects. If allure is "the separation between objects," then wonder is the separation between objects and allure itself.[16] Wonder is a way objects orient.

Yet wonder has been all but eviscerated in modern thought, left behind as a naive delusion. When we approach objects as social relativists, they bear interest only as products or regulators of human behavior and society. This is how *The Wire* treats cinderblocks, Chicken McNuggets, freighter ships, and graffiti—such things bear interest only when they advance some perspective on human behavior. But when we approach objects as scientific naturalists, the same prejudice applies. Sure, the butterfat crystals and the flour protein levels enter the conversation, but only insofar as they facilitate the creation of a better cake, one crafted for human enjoyment. Even though some scientists might try to deny the human-centricity of science itself, arguing that it seeks instead to uncover universal truths about the universe, the rhetoric of science is entirely and totally obsessed with human knowledge, action, and use.

DISMANTLING

There is no better place to track this phenomenon than in recent debates about science, technology, engineering, and math (STEM) education. As the story goes, a globalized economy has put pressure on the United States, which has allowed its scientific leadership to wane. This challenge, we are told, puts America's status as economic and intellectual world leader at risk, as nations like India and China train more scientists and engineers in greater number and at higher competence. The data support this position: for example, the 2005 National Assessment of Educational Progress reported that 61 percent of high school seniors achieved basic competence in mathematics, while only 23 percent performed at a proficient level.[17] The number of jobs that require science and engineering training, we are told, continues to grow, even as the number of students preparing for these jobs through undergraduate or advanced study is declining. Engineering jobs increased by 159 percent in the two decades ending at the turn of the millennium, but by 2003 there were 1.3 million such jobs unfilled—or being filled by qualified foreign workers, particularly those from India, China, and Germany.[18]

A host of education programs have emerged as a result, most driven by national funding agencies interested in staving off our assured self-destruction. We have the For Inspiration and Recognition of Science and Technology (or FIRST) program, which runs robotics competitions for all age groups.[19] There's Crayons to CAD, a middle-school curriculum meant to increase students' awareness of architectural and construction careers.[20] There's Project Lead the Way, a middle- and high-school curriculum designed to increase the diversity and number of future engineers and technical professionals.[21] I could list many, many more. Among them, in fact, I might cite one of the degree programs at Georgia Tech, in which I teach. Here's an excerpt from our website:

> The Bachelor of Science in Computational Media (BSCM) was developed in recognition of computing's significant role in communication and expression. The BSCM curriculum gives students a grasp of the computer as a medium: the technical, the historical-critical, and the applied. Students gain significant hands-on and theoretical knowledge of computing, as well as an understanding of visual design and the history of media. Our graduates are uniquely positioned to plan, create, and critique new digital media forms for entertainment, education and business.[22]

When asked the excruciatingly unfair question "What do you want to be when you grow up?" children sometimes respond with answers like "bus driver" or "janitor." Adults tend to recoil from such suggestions, thanks to the low economic and social aspiration of professions like these. I remember drawing an intricate portrait of a garbage truck for a first-grade assignment of this sort. I was fascinated by the weird, magical apparatus, with its lumbering gait and suburban roar and pregnant steel rump. But this was during the Cold War, in a private school at which many of the children of Sandia Labs nuclear physicists and rocket sled engineers matriculated. Waste collection was not an appropriate goal. Mercifully, I opted for a much more sensible career as a videogame theorist.

Still, even the more "acceptable" professional goals like astronaut or chef speak less to a child's latent interest in astrophysics or chemistry and more to a state of natural wonder at the alien mystery of objects. But alas, common wisdom in STEM goals suggests that these moments of childhood opportunity must be captured and exploited. For example, a child whose curiosity is piqued by Honda's humanoid robot ASIMO might expect to be deluged with any of a number of possible "next steps" on his or her way to a rewarding and lucrative career in robotics. Whether through books like *The Way Things Work*, which explains the mechanical innards of objects, or through informal tinkering with a Lego Mindstorms kit, or through formal programs like FIRST Robotics, Junior's astonishment is sure to be slowly siphoned out of the tank of wonder, which fuels only the pointless propeller of the schoolboy beanie, in order to fill the cold tank of the machine of progress, a device connected to the gears of society and culture.[23] Despite its claims for universalism, science also has embraced correlationism, always focused on human concerns.

In this sense, science and philosophy are alike in their dealings with wonder. For them, wonder is a void, the opening for a tunnel that leads somewhere more viable. It is a means.

Consider an example. As I've already revealed, I sometimes enjoy the luxury of teaching about the Atari.[24] It is more than three decades old, this weird microcomputer, and one might face difficulty justifying such a lesson in today's educational and professional environment. I have many answers to such charges, more for the press than for the students or administrators. My students learn about the device's silicon components in intricate detail, including the MOS Technologies 6502 microprocessor and the custom-designed Television Interface Adapter. They study the operation of these components to understand how different videogames work, as well as to gain insight into how they were created. And they also learn to program the system for the same reasons, to investigate the creative possibilities of this system, despite its apparent obsolescence, in the same way that a photographer might explore the view camera or a poet the cinquain.

The Atari is dismantled, and new objects present themselves: microprocessor, RAM, audio/video processor, RF signal encoder, objects allowed to resonate and hum weirdly, like the first grader's garbage truck.

But then the mastery of these devices also becomes subject to scrutiny. The 6502 is an antiquated and rudimentary microprocessor with limited application in today's computing systems. And as I discussed in the context of carpentry, the TIA was custom-designed for the Atari, and any knowledge gained of its strange way of rendering a television picture line by line bears no particular utility on contemporary machines like the Xbox or PlayStation.

For this charge too there are answers, answers that redirect the native wonder one experiences in the face of these aggregated transistors into more pragmatic terrain. The 6502, I can argue, is a simple microprocessor that can be easily learned and quickly mastered. As such, it offers an ideal introduction to assembly coding, a skill that one might use when programming a modern microprocessor in machine language, for example, to optimize the performance of inner loops. As for the TIA, it offers unusual inscriptive demands that force a designer to consider creativity in the context of material constraints—potential acts of carpentry. While a budding programmer is unlikely to experience another hardware architecture limited to two 8-bit movable objects per scan line, he or she is quite likely to encounter equally absurd and seemingly arbitrary constraints on modern computers, such as embedded systems. Through logics like these, the Atari shifts its status from garbage truck to humanoid robot.

But what's lost in this rhetorical process? The 6502 microprocessor and TIA graphics chip are ontologically de-emphasized, allowed only a relational role as things in a larger network: the evolution of computing, low-level systems programming, pedagogies of the practice of fundamentals, professional skill development regimens, and so forth. Yet the 6502 is just as wondrous as the cake or the quark. Not for what it *does* but for what it *is*. We could say the same of far more abstract objects mustered in the interest of STEM education.

In the spring of 2010, an issue of *Forbes* magazine featured meditations written for "Your Life in 2020," by thought leaders from the business and intellectual community. Among them was John Maeda, who had just assumed the presidency of the Rhode Island School of Design (RISD). Maeda made a career of artistic computation during his long tenure at the MIT Media Lab. He penned the influential book *Design by Numbers*, an approach to design-minded programming that inspired Ben Fry and Casey Reas's Processing project, a "software sketchbook" for doing interactive visual design in code.[25] In his *Forbes* meditation on life a decade hence, Maeda suggested that STEM ought to be expanded to "STEAM." The "A" would stand for Art:

> But if technology and the ability to be connected disappear further into the background, what will occupy our foreground? A bit of the humanity we've always valued in the "real world." Legislators who are currently fixated on STEM (Science, Technology, Engineering and Math) education as the key to innovation will realize that STEM needs some STEAM—some art in the equation. We'll witness a return to the integrity of craft, the humanity of authorship, and the rebalancing of our virtual and physical spaces. We'll see a 21st-century renaissance in arts- and design-centered approaches to making things, where you—the individual—will take center stage in culture and commerce.[26]

On the one hand, it's hard to object to Maeda's suggestion; surely he's right that the STEM obsession seeps from the ice floes of a glacial inhumanity. But on the other hand, the addition of art to the mix doesn't particularly enhance the missing focus on things themselves. In Maeda's account, art becomes a lubricant for science and engineering output, a valve through which its application can be made resonant with human practice.[27] As in the popular reading of Plato and Aristotle, wonder becomes an intentional curiosity, the equivalent of Martin Heidegger's *care (Sorge)*.

But what if the real obstacle to youthful interest in science arises not from a distaste for mathematics or the natural world but from a latent dissatisfaction with the way science melts the shell of wonder around ordinary objects? Science, like philosophy, has assumed that wonder is always a type of puzzlement, an itch meant to be scratched so we can get on with things. But, for the child, a computer or a robot or a cake or a definite integral is not merely a wellspring for a possible future career, or even a vessel for play, work, sustenance, or measurement. It's an object worthy of consideration for its own sake, a thing of wonder, like Iris's rainbow, suspended between the pique of intrigue and the utility of application. To acknowledge the garbage truck as object is to acknowledge the real object that isolates, while refusing to hold that it must always connect to any other in a network of relations.

Perhaps the new shoots of a solution can be found in Maistre's interpretation of Bacon's "broken knowledge," the "science attached to nothing." This unattached knowledge does not mean that larger systems of thought cannot be applied multiply, but that the subject of broken knowledge also implies an internal systematicity that resists external logics—whether those be physics or metaphysics. The science attached to nothing is the logic of the real object.

The series finale of *The Wire* ends with a montage depicting the fates of its characters. The names of Bodie and Lex find themselves newly applied to the graffiti wall memorial. Herc downs some brews with his Baltimore Police Department colleagues as they celebrate McNulty's retirement. Scott Templeton accepts the Pulitzer Prize. Cascades of confetti cover Carcetti as he celebrates victory in the

FIGURE 8. Creatures play marbles with galaxies in the closing images from Barry Sonnenfeld's film *Men in Black* (1997).

Maryland gubernatorial race. Stan Valchek becomes police commissioner. Edward Tilghman Middle School student "Dukie" Weems injects heroin with the arabber he befriended. Wee-Bey and Chris Partlow bide time in the courtyard of the Maryland State prison. And life goes on in the low-rise housing projects, on the waterfront, and on the streets of Baltimore.

Compare it with the end of the feature film adaptation of the comic book *Men in Black*. Tommy Lee Jones and Will Smith's characters have spent the entire movie attempting to find and then protect "the universe," which is revealed to be a small glass orb hanging like a charm from a cat's collar. The film's final sequence is composed of a rapid outward zoom reminiscent of Charles and Ray Eames's *Powers of Ten*, but accelerated by several factors of ten. We move from the streets of New York out to the city, the continent, the planet, the solar system. Eventually our galaxy is revealed to exist within a glass sphere in the sinewy paw of some alien creature, which wields it in a game of marbles (Figure 8).

The concept is right, but the scale is too large and too small all at once. The two sides of tiny ontology glisten as they flip like a coin: *everything* is like the marble universe in *Men in Black*. Partitioned like so many galaxies, each thing, from leavener bubble to pound cake, from mathematical operand to robotic companion, from opium poppy to criminal justice system, each demands its own broken knowledge. Weird, tiny, totalities simultaneously run their own rules and participate in the dominion of others around them. Each thing remains alien to every other, operationally as well as physically. To wonder is to respect things as things in themselves.

In addition to all the branches of theory and science writ large, then, we also face the opportunity to produce the philosophies and sciences attached to nothing, to use Maistre's term. But unlike these old methods, which strive to illuminate, wonder hopes to darken, to isolate, to insulate. Perhaps this is one signal for the future: instead of roboticists and anthropologists, instead of biomedical engineers and medievalists, we will find alloyers and philopescetes and tacologists. Perhaps, in that future world, versions of the younger me will smile as proud teachers tousle their hair over the wonderful garbage trucks they sketch at their grade-school desks.

THE ALIEN EVERYDAY

Objections to OOO often accuse it of seeing humans as lesser forms than other things, rather than as one of many units on equal footing. The example of objectifying women in the case of the OOO symposium image toy offers but one particularly salient example. In another such discussion, Levi Bryant worries over Nathan A. Gale's comparison of OOO and zombies:

> The reason I get nervous about the suggestion that OOO necessarily encounters the figure of the zombie . . . is that already in the debates that have raged around OOO and SR [speculative realism], there have been continuous charges of "objectifying" humans, which I think the zombie image all too easily plays into.[28]

His clarification strikes a nerve, because it reminds me of the challenges Nick Montfort and I have had in advocating for platform studies, our approach to (and book series on) computing systems and creativity.[29] The platform studies project is an example of alien phenomenology. Yet our efforts to draw attention to hardware and software objects have been met with myriad accusations of human erasure: technological determinism most frequently, but many other fears and outrages about "ignoring" or "conflating" or "reducing," or otherwise doing violence to "the cultural aspects" of things.

This is a myth.[30] In our treatment of computer hardware, Montfort and I devote considerable attention to matters of business, culture, society, reception, and so forth. But we also pay attention to all the other real things that cultural studies tends to ignore, in this case the construction and operation of particular computer systems, and why they work the way they do. The idea that one could put nonhuman objects in front, even if just for a moment, signals a coarse and sinful inhumanism. It's the same problem that drives Bryant's worry about Gale's zombie talk.

Ironically, OOO offers precisely the opposite opportunity. As Bryant puts it, OOO "allows for the possibility of a new sort of humanism," in which, as Harman adds, "humans will be liberated from the crushing correlational system."[31] For his part, Nick Srnicek offers opprobrium in place of optimism:

> Do we really need another analysis of how a cultural representation does symbolic violence to a marginal group? This is not to say that this work has been useless, just that it's become repetitive. In light of all that, speculative realism provides the best means for creative work to be done, and it provides genuine excitement to think that there are new argumentative realms to explore.[32]

Are we so cowardly as to think expressing interest in things embezzles the last of some limited resource of concern for other humans? If that's what "humanism" has come to mean, then a new conception of it is in order. Just as eating only oysters becomes gastronomically monotonous, so talking only about human behavior becomes intellectually monotonous. The rise of objects need not be a revolution, at least not all the time. This is not just a rise of fists, but also a rise of bodies, as if to leave a table, politely folding one's napkin before departing. Like Bartleby, we can simply declare, "I would prefer not to."

In one of his many defenses of the multitude of actants, Latour offers this rejoinder: "We do not suffer from the lack of a soul. We suffer, on the contrary, from too many troubled souls that have never been offered a decent burial."[33] The bestiary of the undead will no doubt come to mind: not just Nathan Gale's ghosts and zombies but also vampires and mummies, draugar and liches. The Roswell alien might rear its head, too, that humanoid victim left to be molested, preserved, and filed away by government agents. But we could add innumerable members to this list, this list of aliens waiting to be unfettered: quarks, Elizabeth Bennett, single-malt scotch, Ford Mustang fastbacks, lychee fruit, love affairs, dereferenced pointers, Care Bears, sirocco winds, the Tri-City Mall, tort law, the Airbus A330, the five-hundred-drachma note.

In the face of the undead, we exhibit terror. Troubled souls seek relief, silence, release. They operate by broken logics, ones recognizable as neither alive nor dead but striving for one or the other. We fear them because we have no idea what they might do next. Idealisms amount to undead ontologies, metaphysics in which nothing escapes the horrific rift from being, leaving behind a slug's trail of identity politics.

Despite all the science fictional claims to the contrary, the alien is different. One does not ask the alien, "Do you come in peace?" but rather, "What am I to you?" The posture one takes before the alien is that of curiosity, of wonder. For too long, humanists have relinquished wonder to the natural sciences, and then swooped in ostentatiously to blame its awe on false consciousness. The return to realism in metaphysics is also a return to wonder, wonder unburdened by pretense or deception. Let's leave rigor to the dead. Let's trade furrows for gasps. Let's rub our temples at one another no longer. Let's go outside and dig in the dirt.

The alien isn't in the Roswell military morgue, or in the galactic far reaches, or in the undiscovered ecosystems of the deepest sea and most remote tundra. It's *everywhere*. In place of the correlationist's idealist stipulation, we can propose a new realist codicil to append liberally, like hot sauce on chicken wings: *meanwhile*. What else is there, here, anywhere right now? Anything will do, so long as it reminds us of the awesome plenitude of the alien everyday.

> *the wind still blows over*
> *Savannah*
> *and in the Spring*
> *the turkey buzzard struts and*
> *flounces before his*
> *hens.*
>
> —Charles Bukowski

ACKNOWLEDGMENTS

I am grateful to a number of individuals who provided feedback, encouragement, and opportunity during the development of this book.

For their support, guidance, and inspiration: Graham Harman, Levi Bryant, and Tim Morton. For feedback, helpful conversations, and new directions: Michael Austin, Katherine Behar, Jeffrey Bell, Nathan Brown, Hugh Crawford, Wendy Hui Kyong Chun, Patricia Clough, Carl DiSalvo, Melanie Doherty, Paul Ennis, Alex Galloway, Peter Gratton, Katherine Hayles, Eleanor Kaufman, Frenchy Lunning, Tod Papageorge, Anne Pollock, Sean Reid, Barbara Stafford, Steven Shaviro, Bart Simon, TL Taylor, Eugene Thacker, Iain Thomson, and Adam Zaretsky.

I benefited greatly from the opportunity to present versions of this and related work at conferences and symposia, and I am grateful to the organizers of several such meetings for their invitations, logistics, funding, and publicity: to Stephan Günzel, Michael Leibe, and Dieter Mersch (for the invitation to keynote the 2008 Philosophy of Computer Games conference); to Tanya Krzywinska, Helen Kennedy, and Barry Atkins (for the invitation to keynote the 2009 Digital Games Research Association conference); to Carol Colatrella (for the invitation to keynote the 2009 Society for Literature, Science, and the Arts conference); to Ken Knoespel and Jay Telotte (for making funding available for the first Object Oriented Ontology symposium, April 2010); to Liz Losh (for the invitation to present at the symposium Time Will Tell, but Epistemology Won't: In Memory of Richard Rorty, May 2010); to Ken Reinhard and Julia Lupton (for organizing the second Object Oriented Ontology symposium, December 2010); to Roland Faber, Andrew Goffey, and Jeremy Fackenthal (for the invitation to speak at the Whitehead Research Project conference Metaphysics and Things, December 2010); to Katherine Behar (for organizing the two Object Oriented Feminism panels at the 2010 Society for Literature, Science, and the Arts conference); and to McKenzie Wark (for hosting the third Object-Oriented Ontology symposium, September 2011).

NOTES

1. ALIEN PHENOMENOLOGY

1. See http://cryptome.org/eyeball/kumsc-eyeball/kumsc-eyeball.htm.

2. Berlitz and Moore, *Roswell Incident*.

3. They now have their own array, the Allen Telescope Array, or ATA, named for benefactor and Microsoft cofounder Paul Allen. I find it almost impossible not to misread "Alien Telescope Array."

4. The last eruption is estimated at 52,000–68,000 years ago. See http://www.nps.gov/cavo/geology.htm.

5. See http://www.nasa.gov/mission_pages/shuttle/shuttlemissions/archives/sts-3.html.

6. Meillassoux, *After Finitude*, 5.

7. Ibid., 13.

8. Latour, *We Have Never Been Modern*, 1–12, 104–7.

9. In fact, Brassier and Meillassoux have since abandoned the term.

10. This sort of event bears some similarity to Alain Badiou's unusual understanding of that term, as a rupture in the state of things, to which one remains faithful. Yet speculative realism is also an event in the ordinary sense of the word, a gathering that took place, that people attended, that appeared on calendars, on flyers, and in email inboxes.

11. Harman, *Tool-Being*, 49.

12. Heidegger, *Being and Time*, 344.

13. Harman, *Guerrilla Metaphysics*, 26, 49.

14. Thanks to Tim Morton for this pronunciation, which is far more sonorous than the inquisitive "oooh."

15. This description is derived from the one I wrote for the first Object Oriented Ontology symposium, which was held April 23, 2010, at the Georgia Institute of Technology. See http://ooo.gatech.edu for descriptions and audio proceedings.

16. Harman, "Realism without Materialism." See also Harman's com-

ments in a thread on Levi Bryant's blog, http://larvalsubjects.wordpress.com/
2009/05/16/realism-through-the-eyes-of-anti-realism/. Braver's account can
be found in *Thing of This World*, xix, 14–23.

17. The fact that there are some Whiteheadian quantum physicists who
hold that actual occasions are akin to subatomic particles offers one example
of why this is a problem for OOO. See, for example, Eastman and Keeton,
Physics and Whitehead, 47–54.

18. Latour, *Pasteurization of France*, 206.

19. Foreman, *Confessions of an Eco-Warrior*, 2–3.

20. Latour, *Politics of Nature*, 20.

21. Weisman, *World without Us*.

22. Nash and Broglio, "Introduction to the Special Issue," 3.

23. http://twitter.com/shaviro/status/4038354360.

24. Pollan, *Botany of Desire*.

25. Whitehead, *Adventures of Ideas*, 220, 234.

26. Griffin, *Unsnarling the World Knot*, 78.

27. Morton, *Ecological Thought*, 28.

28. Ibid.

29. Harman, *Guerrilla Metaphysics*, 91–93.

30. Harman, "On Vicarious Causation," 202.

31. DeLanda, *Intensive Science and Virtual Philosophy*, 152–53, 216.

32. Bryant, *Democracy of Objects*, 33.

33. Ibid.

34. Bogost, *Unit Operations*, 6.

35. Snow, *Two Cultures*, 180–81.

36. Turing, "Computing Machinery and Intelligence," 433–60.

37. Ibid., 433.

38. Searle, "Minds, Brains, and Programs," 417–56.

39. Hodges, *Alan Turing*, quoted in Hayles, *How We Became Posthuman*, xii.

40. Ibid., 423–24.

41. Bryant, *Democracy of Objects*, 44.

42. Ibid., 26, 33.

43. Latour, *Reassembling the Social*, 46.

44. Latour, *We Have Never Been Modern*, 2.

45. Law, "Making a Mess with Method."

46. Ibid., 11.

47. Popławski, "Radial Motion into an Einstein–Rosen Bridge," 110–13.
Popławski's work responds to Lee Smolin's theoretical suggestion that each
black hole contains an entire universe.

48. Harman, *Guerrilla Metaphysics*, 95.

49. Bryant, *Democracy of Objects*, 215.

50. Morton, *Realist Magic*.

51. Bogost, *Unit Operations*, 5.

52. Indeed, Latour makes this comparison more explicit in his essay "From Realpolitik to Dingpolitik—or How to Make Things Public." Says Latour: "A few years ago, computer scientists invented the marvelous expression of 'object-oriented' software to describe a new way to program their computers. We wish to use this metaphor to ask the question, 'What would an *object-oriented* democracy look like?'" The piece was originally written as an introduction to the exhibition catalog *Making Things Public—Atmospheres of Democracy*, which was coedited by Latour and Peter Weibel and published by MIT Press in 2005. That book is out of print, and the essay can now be found either in Fiona Candlin and Raiford Guins's anthology *The Object Reader* (Routledge, 2009) or online at http://www.bruno-latour. fr/articles/article/96-DINGPOLITIK2.html. The above citation can be found in the former book on page 154.

53. Harman, *Guerrilla Metaphysics*, 90.

54. Brown, "Thing Theory," 1.

55. Ibid., 7.

56. Harman makes a similar observation in "On Vicarious Causation": "Elsewhere I have used the phrase 'every relation is itself an object,' and still regard this statement as true. But since this article has redefined relations to include containment, sincerity, and contiguity, the slogan must be reworded as follows: 'every connection is itself an object'" (207).

57. See Bogost, *Unit Operations*, 4–5.

58. Ibid., 7.

59. See Bogost, *Unit Operations*, esp. chaps. 5, 6, 9.

60. Ibid., 10–11.

61. Badiou, "Politics and Philosophy," 130.

62. Hallward, *Badiou*, 333.

63. Badiou, *L'être et l'évenement*, 408.

64. Badiou, *Being and Event*, 13, 26.

65. Lingis, *Imperative*, 63; my emphasis.

66. My exact words are these: "Perhaps the closest philosophical precedent for unit operations is contemporary philosopher Alain Badiou's application of set theory to ontology" (Bogost, *Unit Operations*, 10).

67. Graham Harman makes a similar comparison here: http://doctor zamalek2.wordpress.com/2010/08/04/brief-response-to-vitale/, although he explains the relation of deduction in terms of his theory of the split object (the real object recedes, the sensual object does not).

68. Meillassoux, *After Finitude*, 29, 64.

69. Heinlein, *Grumbles from the Grave*, 49.

70. Husserl, *Husserliana* (24), 118.

71. Lingis, *Imperative*, 63.

72. Zahavi, *Husserl's Phenomenology*, 45.

73. Harman, *Guerrilla Metaphysics*, 183.

74. http://earthspeaks.seti.org.

75. http://earthspeaks.seti.org/pages/About.

76. Rescher, "Extraterrestrial Science," 83–116.

77. Waldenfels, *Phenomenology of the Alien*, 74.

2. ONTOGRAPHY

1. I am indebted to Graham Harman for pointing out this reference, from which we have both benefited in different ways.

2. Harman, "Ontography."

3. Kitschener, *World View of Contemporary Physics*, 76.

4. Lynch, "Ontography," 9.

5. Schulten, *Geographical Imagination in America*, 75.

6. Ibid., 105–6.

7. For example, in the 1970s Caterpillar made use of a controlled English known as Caterpillar Technical English for technical authoring and international documentation. See Kamprath, Adolphson, Mitamura, and Nyberg, "Controlled Language for Multilingual Document Production."

8. Kuhn, "How to Evaluate Controlled Natural Languages." See also http://attempto.ifi.uzh.ch/site/docs/ontograph/.

9. For an example of IKEA assembly instructions, see http://semitough. files.wordpress.com/2008/03/ikea_instructions.jpg. For a different but related example, see Mike Sacks and Julian Sancton's hilarious send-up of IKEA instructions on page 62 of the June 2006 issue of *Esquire*, http://www. doobybrain.com/wp-content/uploads/2008/06/ikea-instructions.jpg.

10. Meillassoux, *After Finitude*, 7, 26–29, 63.

11. Latour, *Pasteurization of France*, 199.

12. Harman, *Guerrilla Metaphysics*, 3.

13. Latour, *Pasteurization of France*, 194.

14. Ibid., 192, 196, 198.

15. Harman, *Guerrilla Metaphysics*, 1.

16. Harman, *Prince of Networks*, 58.

17. Harman, *Guerrilla Metaphysics*, 3.

18. Harman, *Prince of Networks*, 102.

19. Spufford, *Chatto Book of Cabbages and Kings*, 1.

20. Ibid., 2.

21. Ibid., 7.

22. Barthes, *Roland Barthes*, 116–17.

23. Homer, *Iliad*, 2.494–759.

24. Melville, *Moby-Dick*, 294.

25. Another, similar ad appeared in 1986. The "Coke Is It!" campaign itself began in 1982. The two ads can be found at http://www.youtube.com/watch?v=bR7Wj9qnwaM and http://www.youtube.com/watch?v=3zFPc WsmH1g, respectively.

26. See http://www.youtube.com/watch?v=OdB7GDZY3Pk. Carl Willat's website is http://www.carlsfinefilms.com. Lyrics are copyright 2009 by Carl Willat.

27. Blanciak, *Siteless*, 4–5.

28. Lynch, "Ontography," 7.

29. Shore's photographic selectiveness was partly constrained by the high cost of 8x10 plates.

30. Prints can be found in Lange, Fried, and Sternfeld, *Stephen Shore*, 10, 82. The first two examples were earlier images captured with a smaller Rollei instead of the larger view cameras discussed above.

31. Cotter, "A World unto Itself."

32. Ibid., 11.

33. Ibid., 87.

34. Harman, *Quadruple Object*, 124.

35. Ibid., 125.

36. Walton, *Technical Data Requirements*, 170.

37. For more on the tight coupling of skin and mechanics, see Bogost, *Persuasive Games*, 40–51.

38. Good, "All 22,802 Words in Scribblenauts."

39. A complete list of merits can be found at http://www.scribblenauts guide.com/page/Scribblenauts+Merits.

40. Totilo, "16 Attempts at Scribblenauts."

41. Aristotle, *Physics*, book 5.

3. METAPHORISM

1. Latour, *Pasteurization of France*, 215.

2. Nagel, "What Is It Like to Be a Bat?" 435–50. The question was originally posed by the physicalist critic Timothy Sprigge, although Nagel made it famous.

3. Indeed, the molecular process by which the sensation of sweetness occurs remains somewhat mysterious, and a subject of considerable inquiry in contemporary organic chemistry.

4. Nagel, "What Is It Like to Be a Bat?" 436.

5. Ibid., 438.

6. Ibid., 442.

7. Ibid., 439.

8. Ibid., 447.

9. Ibid., 449.

10. Ibid.

11. Bennett, *Vibrant Matter*, 120.

12. Ibid., 438.

13. Harman, *Guerrilla Metaphysics*, 3.

14. Ibid., 150.

15. Ibid., 98.

16. Ibid., 94.

17. Epstein, Genis, and Vladiv-Glover, *Russian Postmodernism*, 105.

18. Quoted in Epstein, Genis, and Vladiv-Glover, *Russian Postmodernism*, 138.

19. Epstein, Genis, and Vladiv-Glover, *Russian Postmodernism*, 106.

20. Zhdanov, "Oblast' nerazmennogo vladen'ia . . . ," 63. Quoted in Epstein, Genis, and Vladiv-Glover, *Russian Postmodernism*, 138.

21. Harman, *Guerrilla Metaphysics*, 153. "Real object" is a technical term for Harman, who splits entities into the withdrawn, real objects and the "sensual objects" that enter into relation.

22. Epstein, *After the Future*, 41.

23. Husserl, *Husserliana* (19), 437.

24. From my own tests: at ISO 200, color and saturation shifts are not noticeable; at ISO 400, red shifts toward yellow by about 17 degrees. Green shifts toward cyan slightly and desaturates by around 20 percent; at ISO 800, red shifts toward yellow by about 28 degrees. Green shifts away from cyan slightly, perhaps by 5 degrees, but desaturates almost entirely.

25. Maurer, "Reality and Digital Pictures."

26. From the question and answer session in a presentation of work at MIT in 1974. The University of California, Riverside has archived an audio recording of the session at http://cmplab16.ucr.edu/podcasts/2008.0009.0003/UCR_CMP_Podcasts_CollectionsSeries2.m4a. I am grateful to Ted Papageorge for sharing this recording with me.

27. http://twitter.com/ibogost/status/5928090585.

28. Latour, *We Have Never Been Modern*, 89.

29. Latour, *Pasteurization of France*, 197.

30. Ibid., 227.

31. Levinas, *Time and the Other*, 90.

32. Morton, "Unsustaining."

33. Ibid.

34. Pollan, *Botany of Desire*, 5.

35. *Husserl* (19), 670.

36. Marcus, *Age of Wire and String*, 37.

37. Ibid., 39.

38. Ibid., 41.

39. Ibid., 40.

40. Hawking, *Brief History of Time*, 1.

4. CARPENTRY

1. "What's The Story? Writers Reveal Why They Write." A transcript can be found at http://www.npr.org/templates/transcript/transcript.php?storyId=128849596.

2. Ibid. I've taken a few liberties in editing the transcript into this context to make it more legible, but these changes are not material; they serve only to make Eubanks's spoken prose clearer in this written context.

3. Ibid.

4. Ibid., with modification, of course.

5. Cf. Diamond, *Guns, Germs, and Steel*.

6. Wood, "Slightest Sardine."

7. Morris, "Academic Cliche Watch." I am grateful to Morris, Alice Daer, and Robert Jackson for discussing this subject with me in late August 2010 (cf. http://www.bogost.com/blog/academic_mumblespeak.shtml).

8. Bryant, "You Know You're a Correlationist If . . ."

9. Ibid.

10. Rorty, "Comments on Marjorie Green's A Philosophical Testament," 4–5.

11. Ihde, *Experimental Phenomenology*, 14.

12. Crawford, *Shop Class as Soulcraft*, 199.

13. Thomson, *Heidegger on Ontotheology*, 164.

14. Lingis, *Community of Those Who Have Nothing in Common*, 41; Harman, *Guerrilla Metaphysics*, 2, 72, 166.

15. Latour, *Pasteurization of France*, 205–6.

16. See http://www.mediawiki.org.

17. As of September 2010, Wikipedia contains approximately 3.4 million articles in English. The random article feature can be accessed by loading http://en.wikipedia.org/wiki/Special:Random.

18. The working *Latour Litanizer* can be found at http://www.bogost.com/blog/latour_litanizer.shtml.

19. See http://ooo.gatech.edu.

20. I am indebted to Levi Bryant for this particular turn of phrase.

21. Montfort and Bogost, *Racing the Beam*, 14–17, 145–50.

22. Fry, *Deconstructulator*.

23. Hewitt, *Firebug*.

24. See http://awarehome.imtc.gatech.edu/about-us.

25. Romero, Pousman, and Mateas, "Tableau Machine: An Alien Presence in the Home," 1265–66.

26. Ibid., 1266.

27. Ibid., 1267.

28. Ibid., 1266.

29. Ibid., 1267.

30. Pousman, Romero, Smith, and Mateas, "Living with Tableau Machine," 375.

31. Ibid.

32. Bennett, *Vibrant Matter*, 120.

33. Meyer, "Introduction," 8.

34. Whitehead, *Process and Reality*, 259. Quoted in Meyer, 9.

35. Latour, *Pasteurization of France*, 219.

36. Ibid., 218.

37. Urustar, *Urustar*.

38. Galloway, "Guy Debord's 'Kriegspiel.'"

39. His cookbook, *The Whole Beast: Nose to Tail Eating*, contains recipes nearly impossible to follow, not because of complexity but because the requisite types and parts of the animals they contain are nearly impossible to find. Ox tongue, pig blood, lamb's brains, pig spleen. Even the staunchest of vegetarians can appreciate *The Whole Beast*, for it is much more than just an essay on the lost thrift and wanton wastefulness of modern carnivorous life; it is also an experiment in the textures, functions, and sheer existence of things unseen: duck necks, sheep hearts, bone marrow.

40. See http://smartech.gatech.edu/handle/1853/20514. For more on the Mad Housers, see http://www.madhousers.org/.

5. WONDER

1. Lander, *Stuff White People Like*, 34–35.

2. Ibid., 108.

3. Ibid., 109.

4. http://www.citypaper.com/special/story.asp?id=11846.

5. "Tanks, Trucks, and Vikings" (season 5, episode 11), which originally aired on October 2, 2008.

6. Brown, *I'm Just Here for More Food*, 177. See also http://www.npr.org/templates/story/story.php?storyId=4229760.

7. Plato, *Theaetetus*, 155c, in *Collected Dialogues*, 860.

8. Plato, *Theaetetus*, 155d.

9. Butler, *Imagination and Politics in Seventeenth-Century England*, 58.

10. Bacon, "On the Advancement of Learning," in *Works*, 9–10.

11. Maistre, *Examination of the Philosophy of Bacon*, 170.

12. Ibid., 171. A serinette is a device used to teach music to canaries.

13. Bacon, *Works*, 493.

14. Parsons, "Philosophy of Wonder," 85.

15. Harman, "On Vicarious Causation," 215.

16. Ibid.

17. See http://www.edigroupkc.com/TheStemCrisis.htm for many examples.

18. Ibid.

19. See http://wwww.usfirst.org.

20. See http://www.crayonstocad.org.

21. See http://www.pltw.org.

22. http://lcc.gatech.edu/compumedia/?page_id=9.

23. Macaulay, *The Way Things Work*.

24. For two example syllabi, see http://www.bogost.com/teaching/the_atari_video_computer_syste.shtml and http://www.bogost.com/teaching/atari_hacks_remakes_and_demake.shtml.

25. For more on Processing, see http://www.processing.org.

26. Maeda, "Your Life in 2020." I am grateful to Mark Guzdial for making me aware of Maeda's article.

27. This attitude has made for a controversial tenure as president of RISD. See, for example, Macris, "After Criticism."

28. Gale, "Zombies Ate My Ontology"; Bryant, "Imbroglios of Objects."

29. Cf. Montfort and Bogost, *Racing the Beam*. See also http://platformstudies.com.

30. For our complete response, see Bogost and Montfort, "Platform Studies."

31. See http://larvalsubjects.wordpress.com/2009/08/20/imbroglios-of-objects/#comment-19063 and http://larvalsubjects.wordpress.com/2009/08/20/imbroglios-of-objects/#comment-19088, respectively.

32. Ennis, "Interview with Nick Srnicek," http://anotherheideggerblog.blogspot.com/2009/08/interview-with-nick-srnicek.html.

33. Latour, *Pasteurization of France*, 188.

BIBLIOGRAPHY

Aristotle. *Physics*. Trans. Robin Waterfield. Oxford: Oxford University Press, 2008.

Bacon, Francis. "On the Advancement of Learning." In *Works*, vol. 1. London: W. Baynes and Son, 1824.

Badiou, Alain. *L'être et l'évenement*. Paris: Seuil, 1988.

———. "Politics and Philosophy." *Angelaki* 3, no. 3 (1998): 113–33.

Barthes, Roland. *Roland Barthes*. New York: Farrar, Straus and Giroux, 1977.

Bennett, Jane. *Vibrant Matter: A Political Ecology of Things*. Durham, N.C.: Duke University Press, 2010.

Berlitz, Charles, and William L. Moore. *The Roswell Incident*. New York: Grosset and Dunlap, 1980.

Blanciak, François. *Siteless: 1001 Building Forms*. Cambridge, Mass.: MIT Press, 2008.

Bogost, Ian. *Persuasive Games: The Expressive Power of Videogames*. Cambridge, Mass.: MIT Press, 2007.

———. *Unit Operations: An Approach to Videogame Criticism*. Cambridge, Mass.: MIT Press, 2006.

Bogost, Ian, and Nick Montfort. "Platform Studies: Frequently Questioned Answers." *Proceedings of the Digital Arts and Cultures Conference*, December 12–15, 2009, Irvine, California.

Braver, Lee. *A Thing of This World: A History of Continental Anti-Realism*. Chicago: Northwestern University Press, 2007.

Brown, Alton. *I'm Just Here for More Food*. New York: Stewart, Tabori, and Chang, 2004.

Brown, Bill. "Thing Theory." *Critical Inquiry* 28 (Autumn 2001): 1–22.

Bryant, Levi. *The Democracy of Objects*. Ann Arbor, Mich.: Open Humanities, 2011.

———. "Imbroglios of Objects." *Larval Subjects.* August 20, 2009. http://larvalsubjects.wordpress.com/2009/08/20/imbroglios-of-objects.

———. "You Know You're a Correlationist If . . ." *Larval Subjects.* July 30, 2010. http://larvalsubjects.wordpress.com/2010/07/30/you-know-youre-a-correlationist-if/.

Butler, Todd Wayne. *Imagination and Politics in Seventeenth-Century England.* Surrey, U.K.: Ashgate, 2008.

Candlin, Fiona, and Raiford Guins, eds. *The Object Reader.* New York: Routledge, 2009.

Cotter, Suzanne. "A World unto Itself." Aspen Art Museum. http://www.aspenartmuseum.org/shore_cotter.html.

DeLanda, Manuel. *Intensive Science and Virtual Philosophy.* London: Continuum, 2005.

Derrida, Jacques. *Glas.* Trans. John P. Leavy Jr. and Richard Rand. Lincoln: University of Nebraska Press, 1990.

Diamond, Jared. *Guns, Germs, and Steel.* New York: Norton, 1997.

Eastman, Timothy E., and Hank Keeton. *Physics and Whitehead: Quantum, Process, and Experience.* Albany: State University of New York Press, 2003.

Ennis, Paul. "Interview with Nick Srnicek." *Another Heidegger Blog.* August 13, 2009. http://anotherheideggerblog.blogspot.com/2009/08/interview-with-nick-srnicek.html.

Epstein, Mikhail. *After the Future: The Paradoxes of Postmodernism and Contemporary Russia.* Trans. Anesa Miller-Pogacar. Amherst: University of Massachusetts Press, 1995.

Epstein, Mikhail, Aleksandr Genis, and Slobodanka Vladiv-Glover. *Russian Postmodernism: New Perspectives on Post-Soviet Culture.* London: Berghahn Books, 1999.

Foreman, Dave. *Confessions of an Eco-Warrior.* New York: Three Rivers Press, 1993.

Fry, Ben. *Deconstructulator.* November 2003. http://benfry.com/deconstructulator/.

Gale, Nathan A. "Zombies Ate My Ontology." *An Un-Canny Ontology.* August 17, 2009. http://un-cannyontology.blogspot.com/2009/08/zombies-ate-my-ontology.html.

Galloway, Alexander R. "Guy Debord's 'Kriegspiel': Nostalgic Algorithms in Late Modernity." Paper presented at the Modern Language Association Conference, December 27, 2007, Chicago.

Good, Owen. "All 22,802 Words in Scribblenauts." *Kotaku.* September 12, 2009. http://kotaku.com/5358054/all-22802-words-in-scribblenauts.

Griffin, David Ray. *Unsnarling the World Knot: Consciousness, Freedom, and the Mind-Body Problem.* Berkeley: University of California Press, 1998.

Hallward, Peter. *Badiou: A Subject to Truth.* Minneapolis: University of Minnesota Press, 2003.

Harman, Graham. *Guerrilla Metaphysics: Phenomenology and the Carpentry of Things.* Chicago: Open Court, 2005.

———. "On Vicarious Causation." *Collapse: Journal of Philosophical Research and Development* 2 (2007): 187–221.

———. "Ontography: The Rise of Objects." *Object-Oriented Philosophy,* July 14, 2009, http://doctorzamalek2.wordpress.com/2009/07/14/ontography-the-rise-of-objects/.

———. *Prince of Networks: Bruno Latour and Metaphysics.* Melbourne: re:press, 2009.

———. *The Quadruple Object.* Winchester, U.K.: ZerO Books, 2011.

———. "Realism without Materialism." Paper presented at the Twenty-first Century Materialism Workshop, June 20–21, 2009, Zagreb, Croatia. For audio proceedings, see http://materialism.mi2.hr.

———. *Tool-Being: Heidegger and the Metaphysics of Objects.* Chicago: Open Court, 2002.

Hawking, Stephen. *A Brief History of Time.* New York: Bantam, 1988.

Hayles, Katherine. *How We Became Posthuman: Virtual Bodies in Cybernetics, Literature, and Informatics.* Chicago: University of Chicago Press, 1999.

Heidegger, Martin. *Being and Time,* rev. ed. Trans. Joseph Stambaugh. Albany: State University of New York Press, 2010.

Heinlein, Robert. *Grumbles from the Grave.* Ed. Virginia Heinlein. New York: Harmony Books, 1990.

Henderson, Fergus. *The Whole Beast: Nose to Tail Eating.* New York: Ecco, 2004.

Hewitt, Joe. *Firebug,* http://getfirebug.com.

Hodges, Andrew. *Alan Turing: The Enigma of Intelligence.* London: Unwin, 1985.

Homer. *Iliad.* Trans. Robert Fagles. New York: Penguin, 1998.

Husserl, Edmund. *Husserliana: Edmund Husserl Gesammelte Werke* (Logische Untersuchungen). Berlin: Springer Verlag.

Ihde, Don. *Experimental Phenomenology: An Introduction.* Albany: State University of New York Press, 1986.

Johnson, Steven. *Everything Bad Is Good for You: How Today's Popular Culture Is Actually Making Us Smarter.* New York: Riverhead Books, 2005.

Kamprath, Christine, Eric Adolphson, Teruko Mitamura, and Eric Nyberg. "Controlled Language for Multilingual Document Production: Experience with Caterpillar Technical English." In *Proceedings of the Second International Workshop on Controlled Language Applications* (CLAW98). Pittsburgh, Pa.: Language Technologies Institute, Carnegie Mellon University, May 21–22, 1998.

Kitschener, Richard F. *The World View of Contemporary Physics: Does It Need a New Metaphysics?* Buffalo: State University of New York Press, 1988.

Kuhn, Tobias. *Controlled English for Knowledge Representation*. PhD diss., Faculty of Economics, Business Administration, and Information Technology, University of Zurich, 2010. http://attempto.ifi.uzh.ch/site/pubs/papers/doctoral_thesis_kuhn.pdf.

———. "How to Evaluate Controlled Natural Languages." *Pre-Proceedings of the Workshop on Controlled Natural Language* (CNL 2009), *CEUR Workshop Proceedings*, vol. 448 (2009).

Lander, Christian. *Stuff White People Like: A Definitive Guide to the Unique Taste of Millions*. New York: Random House, 2008.

Lange, Christy, Michael Fried, and Joel Sternfeld. *Stephen Shore*. New York: Phaidon, 2007.

Latour, Bruno. "From Realpolitik to Dingpolitik—or How to Make Things Public." In *Making Things Public—Atmospheres of Democracy*, ed. Bruno Latour and Peter Weibel. Cambridge, Mass.: MIT Press, 2005.

———. *The Pasteurization of France*. Trans. Alan Sheridan and John Law. Cambridge, Mass.: Harvard University Press, 1993.

———. *Politics of Nature: How to Bring the Sciences into Democracy*. Cambridge, Mass.: Harvard University Press, 2004.

———. *Reassembling the Social: An Introduction to Actor-Network Theory*. Oxford: Oxford University Press, 2005.

———. *We Have Never Been Modern*. Trans. Catherine Porter. Cambridge, Mass.: Harvard University Press, 1993.

Law, John. "Making a Mess with Method," Centre for Science Studies, Lancaster University, Lancaster, http://www.comp.lancs.ac.uk/sociology/papers/Law-Making-a-Mess-with-Method.pdf.

Levinas, Immanuel. *Time and the Other*. Trans. Richard A. Cohen. Pittsburgh: Duquesne University Press, 1990.

Lingis, Alphonso. *The Community of Those Who Have Nothing in Common*. Bloomington: Indiana University Press, 1994.

Lynch, Michael. "Ontography: Investigating the Production of Things, Deflating Ontology." Paper presented at the Oxford Ontologies Workshop, Saïd Business School, June 25, 2008, Oxford University.

Macaulay, David. *The Way Things Work*. New York: Houghton Mifflin, 1988.

Macris, Gina. "After Criticism, RISD's Maeda Retools His Approach."

Providence Journal. May 15, 2011. http://www.projo.com/education/content/ RISD_MAEDA_05-15-11_4JNUUP6_v47.2cd3700.html.

Maeda, John. *Design by Numbers.* Cambridge, Mass.: MIT Press, 2001.

———. "Your Life in 2020." *Forbes.* April 8, 2010, http://www.forbes.com/ 2010/04/08/john-maeda-design-technology-data-companies-10-keynote. html.

Maistre, Joseph de. *An Examination of the Philosophy of Bacon.* Trans. Richard L. Lebrun. Montreal: McGill-Queen's University Press, 1998.

Marcus, Ben. *The Age of Wire and String.* Champaign, Ill.: Dalkey Archive Press, 1998.

Maurer, Charles. "Reality and Digital Pictures." *TidBITS.* December 12, 2005. http://db.tidbits.com/article/8365.

Meillassoux, Quentin. *After Finitude: An Essay on the Necessity of Contingency.* Trans. Ray Brassier. London: Continuum, 2008.

Melville, Herman. *Moby-Dick, or, The Whale.* New York: Charles Scribner's Sons, 1902.

Meyer, Steven. "Introduction." *Configurations* 13, no. 1 (2005): 1–33.

Montfort, Nick, and Ian Bogost. *Racing the Beam: The Atari Video Computer System.* Cambridge, Mass.: MIT Press, 2008.

Morris, David. "Academic Cliche Watch: '. . . In Particular Ways.'" *Minds Like Knives.* June 16, 2010. http://mindslikeknives.blogspot.com/2010/06/ academic-cliche-watch-in-particular.html.

Morton, Timothy. *The Ecological Thought.* Cambridge, Mass.: Harvard University Press, 2010.

———. *Realist Magic.* Ann Arbor, Mich.: Open Humanities Press, forthcoming.

———. "Unsustaining." *World Picture* 5 (2011). http://english.okstate.edu/ worldpicture.

Nagel, Thomas. "What Is It Like to Be a Bat?" *Philosophical Review* 83, no. 4 (1974): 435–50.

Nash, Richard, and Ron Broglio. "Introduction to the Special Issue: Thinking with Animals." *Configurations* 14, no. 1 (2006): 1–7.

Parsons, Howard L. "A Philosophy of Wonder." *Philosophy and Phenomenological Research* 30, no. 1 (1969): 84–101.

Plato. *The Collected Dialogues of Plato: Including the Letters.* Ed. Edith Hamilton and Huntington Cairns. Princeton, N.J.: Princeton University Press/Bollingen, 2005.

Pollan, Michael. *The Botany of Desire: A Plant's-Eye View of the World.* New York: Random House, 2002.

Popławski, Nikodem J. "Radial Motion into an Einstein–Rosen Bridge," *Physics Letters* 687, nos. 2–3 (2010): 110–13.

Pousman, Zachary, Mario Romero, Adam Smith, and Michael Mateas.

"Living with Tableau Machine: A Longitudinal Investigation of a Curious Domestic Intelligence." *Proceedings of UbiComp '08*, 370–79, September 21–24, 2008, Seoul.

Rescher, Nicholas. "Extraterrestrial Science." Pp. 83–116 in *Extraterrestrials: Science and Alien Intelligence*, ed. Edward Regis Jr. Cambridge: Cambridge University Press, 1985.

Romero, Mario, Zachary Pousman, and Michael Mateas. "Tableau Machine: An Alien Presence in the Home." *Proceedings of CHI 2006*, 1265–66, April 22–27, 2006, Montreal.

Rorty, Richard. "Comments on Marjorie Greene's A Philosophical Testament." Paper presented at the Western Division APA meetings, April 5, 1996, Seattle, Washington. Available in the UC Irvine archives, at http://ucispace.lib.uci.edu/bitstream/handle/10575/748/GRENE.pdf? sequence=1 (authorized access required).

Schulten, Susan. *The Geographical Imagination in America, 1880–1950*. Chicago: University of Chicago Press, 2001.

Searle, John. "Minds, Brains, and Programs." *Behavioral and Brian Sciences* 3, no. 3 (1980): 417–56.

Snow, C. P. *The Two Cultures*. Cambridge: Cambridge University Press, 1960.

Spufford, Francis. *The Chatto Book of Cabbages and Kings: Lists in Literature*. London: Chatto and Windus, 1989.

Thomson, Iain. *Heidegger on Ontotheology: Technology and the Politics of Education*. Cambridge: Cambridge University Press, 2005.

Totilo, Stephen. "16 Attempts at Scribblenauts." *Kotaku*. August 4, 2009. http://kotaku.com/5329596/16-attempts-at-scribblenauts.

Turing, Alan. "Computing Machinery and Intelligence," *Mind* 59, no. 236 (1950): 433–60. http://mind.oxfordjournals.org/cgi/reprint/LIX/236/433.

Urustar. *Urustar: The Game* (self-published, 2009), http://urustar.net.

Waldenfels, Bernhard. *Phenomenology of the Alien*. Trans. Alexander Kozin and Tanja Stähler. Evanston, Ill.: Northwestern University Press, 2011.

Walton, Thomas F. *Technical Data Requirements for Systems Engineering and Support*. New York: Prentice-Hall, 1965.

Weisman, Alan. *The World without Us*. New York: Dunne, 2007.

"What's The Story? Writers Reveal Why They Write." *Talk of the Nation*. National Public Radio, July 29, 2010, Washington, D.C.

Whitehead, Alfred North. *Adventures of Ideas*. New York: Macmillan, 1933.

———. *Process and Reality*. New York: Free Press, 1979.

Whitehead, Alfred North, and Bertrand Russell. *Principia Mathematica*. Cambridge: Cambridge University Press, 1994.

Wood, James. "The Slightest Sardine: Review of *The Oxford English Literary History, Vol. XII: 1960–2000: The Last of England?*" *London Review of Books,* May 2004, 11–12. http://www.lrb.co.uk/v26/n10/james-wood/the-slightest-sardine.

Zahavi, Dan. *Husserl's Phenomenology.* Palo Alto, Calif.: Stanford University Press, 2003.

Zhdanov, Ivan. *Nerazmennoe nebo.* Moscow: Sovremennik, 1990.

INDEX

access, human, 4; philosophies of, 5
Ace of Cakes (television series), 116–18
actants, 8, 10, 39, 133; relations among, 76, 114
actor-network theory, 6, 7, 10, 19–20
Adams, Ansel, 48
Adventure (graphical adventure game), 100
Aethelberht II, 35
ahimsa, Jainist, 73
alien phenomenology, 32–34, 62; artifacts of, 109; carpentry in, 92–104; characterization of experience, 63; distortion in, 66; incompatibility in, 40; source codes in, 105; speculative, 78; wonder in, 124
aliens: communication with, 33–34, 137n3; sightings of, 2
Allen Telescope Array (ATA), 137n3
American Idol (television series), 115
animal rights, 72–73
animal studies, 8
anthropocentrism, 7, 64–65, 80; and correlationism, 29; in meta-phorism, 74, 78; narrative of, 42; among residents of homes, 108

anticorrelationism, 5, 80
apeiron, Anaximandrean, 11
APIs (application programming interfaces), 95; for Flickr, 98; for MediaWiki, 95
architecture: optical illusion in, 46; Wittgenstein's, 99–100
Aristotle: on causation, 75, 78; on *hexis*, 77; *Metaphysics*, 92; on wonder, 121, 122, 123, 129
ASIMO (humanoid robot), 126
Association of Computing Machinery Computer-Human Interaction Conference, 107
Asteroids (computer game), 101
astrobiology, 2
Atari Video Computer System (VCS, aka Atari 2600), 100; components of, 127, 128; creative possibilities of, 127; human interface with, 104; teaching about, 126, 145n24; TIA graphics and sound chip of, 102–4, 127, 128
atomism, Democritean, 11
Aware Home (residence), 106
awe, 120–24

Bacon, Francis: on broken knowledge, 129; on wonder, 122, 123

IAN BOGOST is professor of digital media at the Georgia Institute of Technology, where he is also director of the graduate program in digital media. He is the author of *Unit Operations: An Approach to Videogame Criticism, Persuasive Games: The Expressive Power of Videogames, A Slow Year: Game Poems,* and *How to Do Things with Videogames* (Minnesota, 2010) and coauthor of *Racing the Beam: The Atari Video Computer System* and *Newsgames: Journalism at Play.*